Contents

1	SOCIAL NETWORKS	page 2
2	EXPERTS	page 8
3	SURVIVAL	page 14
	PROGRESS TEST 1, UNITS 1–3	page 20
4	REINVENTION	page 22
5	FOOD FOR THOUGHT	page 28
6	THAT'S ENTERTAINMENT	page 34
	PROGRESS TEST 2, UNITS 4–6	page 40
7	SOCIETY AND YOU	page 42
8	CRIME AND PUNISHMENT	page 48
9	LUCK AND FORTUNE	page 54
	PROGRESS TEST 3, UNITS 7–9	page 60
10	VALUE FOR MONEY	page 62
11	TECHNOLOGY	page 68
12	OUT OF THE ORDINARY	page 74
	PROGRESS TEST 4, UNITS 10–12	page 80
	TRANSCRIPTS	page 82
	TRACK LISTING	page 88

The BIG Picture

B2 UPPER INTERMEDIATE Workbook

ALASTAIR LANE

www.richmondelt.com/thebigpicture

1 Social networks

Vocabulary
Relationships

1 Read the clues and complete the puzzle. What is the hidden word in grey? _____

1. Someone who tells you what to do in your job.
2. You play sports on the same side as this person.
3. Your mother or your father.
4. Someone who you share an apartment with.
5. Someone who you know quite well, but who is not really a friend yet.
6. Someone travelling on public transport.
7. Someone who works in the same company as you.
8. A word for someone in a romantic relationship with you, e.g. a wife, husband, girlfriend or boyfriend.

2 Complete the words.

1. Cassandra is my l __ n __ m __ __ ag __ __ at work. She tells me what work to do.
2. My wife's mum and dad are really nice. It's great when you get on with your p __ r __ __ __ s- __ n-l __ __ __ .
3. I have three really c __ __ __ __ friends and we spend all our time together.
4. I can't afford to rent an apartment on my own so I need to find a f __ __ tm __ __ e.
5. Momoko is my b __ __ __ friend – we're almost like sisters!
6. I'm really enjoying my Chinese course. My c __ __ s __ m __ t __ s are great fun!
7. Laura and Karl have been going out for about two months. They make a great c __ __ p __ __ !
8. I got lost on the way to the party, so I had to ask a p __ __ __ __ __ r- __ __ for directions.

3 Complete the sentences with the expressions from the box. There is one word you don't need.

| colleagues | ex-boyfriend | parents | parents-in-law |
| passer-by | strangers | team-mate | |

1. Your _____ will have very similar DNA to you.
2. I get on well with my _____ – we're still friends, even though we broke up last year.
3. I didn't meet my _____ – my husband's family – until our wedding day.
4. While I was shopping this morning, a _____ stopped me and asked me where I had bought my T-shirt!
5. Alba made loads of good friends in her last job. Her _____ were a lot of fun.
6. I find it difficult to talk to _____ . I never know what to say when I meet people for the first time.

4 Match 1–6 to a–f to make full sentences.

1. If you want Sara to be your girlfriend, you should ____
2. It was a real surprise. I was in the supermarket when I ____
3. Julie and Tim had a big argument and now they've ____
4. Nick and Vince are so annoying – they never ____
5. My new classmates are great. I ____
6. After the game today, the whole team is going to ____

a. got on with them immediately.
b. turn up on time.
c. meet up in the café.
d. split up.
e. ask her out.
f. ran into my old English teacher.

Phrasal verbs

5 Choose the correct option to complete the sentences.

1. You're crazy to *drop / leave* out of school when you're only 17! You need to complete your studies!
2. Dimitri is going to travel around the world on his own. I know he can *look / protect* after himself, but I still worry!
3. I wasn't doing any sports so I *made / took* up running. I really enjoy it now.
4. I don't understand why you and Ximena are arguing. You should *do / make* up and be friends again.
5. Don't worry about our university project. You can *count / number* on me to do my part of the work.
6. We've had a lot of difficulties in our relationship recently, but we've *spoken / talked* them over and everything's OK now.
7. It's Marc's birthday on Sunday so we're going to *go / stay* away to Paris for the weekend.
8. At weekends I usually *fly / hang* out with my friends at the park.

Vocabulary extension
Further phrasal verbs

6 a 🔊 1.1 Listen to two speakers. Who says phrasal verbs a–j, speaker 1 or speaker 2?

a ☐ break down   f ☐ pick up
b ☐ carry on   g ☐ set off
c ☐ give up   h ☐ sort out
d ☐ go off   i ☐ throw away
e ☐ hand in   j ☐ write down

b Match the speakers to the photos.

a ☐

b ☐

7 Listen again. Complete the sentences.
1 We _____ _____ really early in the morning.
2 We _____ _____ my cousin at her house.
3 Suddenly, the car _____ _____ ! It just stopped – in the middle of nowhere!
4 Dad thought he could _____ the problem _____ , but it was too difficult for him.
5 So we just _____ _____ and went home.
6 We were under a lot of pressure because we had to _____ _____ a big project later that day.
7 Suddenly, the fire alarm _____ _____ .
8 The university tests the fire alarms at 3 p.m. every Wednesday. So we _____ _____ working as normal.
9 I was just _____ _____ the last part of the report.
10 Apparently, someone _____ a cigarette _____ while it was still lit.

8 Complete the sentences with the correct form of phrasal verbs from **6a**.
1 They're going on a three-day walk in the mountains. They*'re setting off* early tomorrow morning.
2 What day do we have to _____ the Geography homework _____ to the teacher?
3 My flatmate's alarm clock _____ at 6 a.m. every morning, and it always wakes me up!
4 Tell me what time your train arrives and I will _____ you _____ in my car.
5 It started raining in the middle of the football match, but my team-mates wanted to _____ playing so by the end of the match we were all really cold and wet.
6 The bus _____ on the way to school so we had to get off and walk!
7 Don't _____ the newspaper _____ – I haven't read it yet!
8 Alberto started doing the Sudoku, but he _____ because it was too difficult!
9 _____ the email address _____ on a piece of paper so you don't forget it.
10 Look at these books! There are hundreds of them. We'll need hours to _____ them all _____ .

Bring it together

9 Complete the email with one word in each gap.

Hi Martina,
I'm writing because I need some help! This week I had a meeting with my boss and my line (1)_____ . They told me that I'm in big trouble because I've been using the internet too much in work time. It was because I went to my sister's wedding last week and my new brother-in-law asked me to put the photos online. I don't have time at home, so I do it at work. Unfortunately, I don't get (2)_____ well with one of my colleagues. He saw me using the web and he told everyone that I wasn't working! It's really unfair. I mean, he never hands his work (3)_____ on time, but I don't say anything about that!
Anyway, that's why I need your help. There's one really great photo of both my (4)_____ – my mum and dad look really nice in it. But the photo's in the street, and at the back of the picture there's a (5)_____ -by who is looking at the camera. I want to remove him from the picture, but I don't know how to do it. Can you sort it (6)_____ for me? It's too difficult for me and it's the last photo for the website. Please help! You know you're my (7)_____ friend in the world!
Thanks!
Love,
Elisa

1

GRAMMAR
Auxiliary verbs

1 Complete the short answers.

1. A Are you on Facebook?
   B Yes, we _____ .
2. A Have you changed your profile photo?
   B No, I _____ .
3. A Please will you talk this over with Marie?
   B No, I _____ .
4. A Does Kim use Twitter a lot?
   B Yes, she _____ .
5. A Am I in that photo?
   B No, you _____ .
6. A Did they meet up last night?
   B No, they _____ .

2 a Put the words and phrases in the correct order to make questions.

1. your who best is friend
   _____
2. get on you with boss do your
   _____
3. meet up did who you at the weekend with
   _____
4. is what favourite your website
   _____
5. online you how often put do photos
   _____

b Answer the questions in **2a**.

1. _____
2. _____
3. _____
4. _____
5. _____

3 Correct the sentences. Tick (✓) two correct sentences.

1. I'm meeting up with you later, aren't we?
2. Jing Jing gets on well with her team-mates, don't she?
3. Curtis and Todd didn't turn up for class, did they?
4. You've invited your flatmates, have you?
5. Dan's dropped out of college, isn't he?
6. You like Xana, don't you?
7. Farah and Tom aren't close friends, aren't they?
8. Nina lives with two flatmates, she doesn't?

4 Complete the online interview with one word in each gap (*isn't*, etc. = one word).

> Today's online chat is with technology expert Lupe Valdez. Join us live from 3 p.m.

I Lupe, hi! So, your latest research project examines the way people use the internet. Can you tell us more?

L Hi! Yes, I really (1)_____ believe the way we surf the internet is changing.

I (2)_____ happening?

L Well, originally, people only went online using PCs. Now, many people visit websites using portable devices like mobile phones or iPads.

I Yes, that's really changed things, (3)_____ it?

L Absolutely. It's partly because we now use apps to go online. This means we browse less – we visit the same webpages again and again.

I That's true. I (4)_____ spend less time browsing now that I have an iPhone! I use a lot of apps.

L Well, apps are fun, (5)_____ they? And very useful!

I Definitely. And they (6)_____ do some amazing things. Have you seen Layar?

L No, I (7)_____ .

I It's great. You can take a photo of a restaurant with your phone, then the app gives you reviews of it.

L Cool. I like Bump. You just touch iPhones with someone and then you can share Facebook friends, and other information.

I Sounds great! So what is your conclusion, Lupe?

L Well, the way we surf the internet is changing. People are exploring less because they just use apps to visit the websites they like. I still (8)_____ know if that's a good thing or a bad thing.

I OK, thanks. Now readers – what do you think? Post your comments below.

Past participles

5 Complete the blog post with the correct form of the words from the box. There are two words that you don't need.

> be create design feel finish
> meet speak take tell write

6 a Match 1–5 to a–e to make full sentences.

1. I'm going to the hairdressers to ____
2. He phoned the police because he ____
3. When women get married, they often ____
4. We live on the sixteenth floor so we ____
5. The customs officers stopped her, and she ____

a. have a dress made for them.
b. had his car stolen.
c. had her bag searched.
d. have our windows cleaned by professionals.
e. have my hair cut.

b Which sentences describe

i. a service which someone does for you?
   _____
ii. a bad experience which might happen to you?
   _____

Reflexive pronouns

7 Complete the sentences. Change the words in brackets to the correct reflexive pronouns.

1. Simon hurt _____ when he was playing football. (he)
2. Ricart – you can help _____ to anything from the fridge. (you)
3. I looked at _____ in the mirror. (I)
4. Fiona and Marina introduced _____ to their new colleagues. (they)
5. We taught _____ to speak French from a book. (we)
6. Sally's 14 so she's old enough to look after _____ . (she)
7. Ask every visitor to get _____ a cup of tea or coffee when they arrive. (they)
8. Girls, don't blame _____ for the accident. (you)

New website!

OK, I know I've (1)_____ a lot of posts about this, but it's finally complete! The new website is (2)_____ and it looks fantastic. I think it will make a really big difference to the company. People had (3)_____ me that the old website was difficult to use, but for a long time I didn't listen. I had (4)_____ it myself and I felt proud of my work! But now I'm very glad I did something about it. The new site is totally different: it was (5)_____ by a web designer, and the photos were (6)_____ by a professional photographer, not just my friends! So far, the feedback has (7)_____ really positive – everyone I have (8)_____ to loves the new design. I'd love to know what you think, too – post your comments below!

Posted today at 9.36 a.m.

BRING IT TOGETHER

8 Read the article about a social networking site. Correct the words and phrases in bold. One word is already correct.

Travel buddies

Imagine you want to travel round the world, or spend the summer in Europe, but none of your friends have the time or the money to go with you. No one likes spending all day on their own, (1)**don't they**? If you don't want to travel round by (2)**itself**, why not find a friend on one of the best social networking sites around: travbuddy.com? The site (3)**designed** to help you find a travel companion. Users post their interests and explain where they want to go. It (4)**is become** a huge internet success story, and the site (5)**was award** a Webby (the Oscars of the internet) in 2010. We used the site (6)**themselves** last year during a trip to Indonesia. We met a local guy, and he showed us loads of cool places in his country. He also helped us out a lot when we (7)**made** our flights cancelled on the last day. Of course, as with

any website, you have to be very careful about meeting strangers: always go with a friend and meet new people in a (8)**crowded** area. One other possibility is to go to one of the Travbuddy 'unofficial' meet-ups. Users of the site (9)**have hold** these in lots of different places, and they're a great way to meet people. I wanted to set one up in my home town last year, but then I discovered another person (10)**was already organised** one. So I went along and met some new friends for my next trip... to Mexico!

Skills development

Functional language Small talk

1 Complete the words.

1 At the airport

A Hi, Luis, and welcome to London!
B Thanks, Julie. Nice to meet you at last. Wow, it's really warm today, (1)i_____ it?
A Yeah, it is. I think you've (2)b_____ the hot weather with you from Brazil!
B That's true. It's really hot back home at the moment.
A I went to Brazil once. I was in Salvador for the carnival. It's amazing, isn't it?
B I love Salvador, but I'm not really a big (3)f_____ of the carnival to be (4)h_____ .
A Really? I loved it!

2 On a training course

C So, Daniel, your boss works in Panama, (5)d_____ she? She's the lady with long, dark hair?
D No, my boss is Carlos Gutierrez. He's here today actually.
C Oh, sorry, I must be thinking of someone (6)e_____ .
D It's an easy mistake to make. It's a big company. We sell computers all over the world.
C (7)T_____ of computers, shall we find somewhere to check our emails?
D Sure. (8)W_____ you like to go to the canteen? They have free Wi-Fi there.
C Sounds great!

Listening Listening for gist

1 a 🔊 1.2 Listen to two conversations. Match the conversations to two of the photos.

b In which conversation are the speakers meeting for the first time? _____

2 Listen again. Complete the sentences.
1 Vera is Julieta's _____ .
2 There were _____ students in Julieta's Spanish class.
3 Nick is from _____ .
4 The temperature in Nick's hometown was _____ degrees.
5 Paula has just arrived in _____ .
6 Michaela is an ex_____ of Paula's.
7 Michaela has _____ hair.
8 Michaela was studying _____ .

> **Strategy** The first time you hear an audio, listen for gist (the main idea). Then listen again more carefully for specific information.

Reading
Activating background knowledge

1 a Read the title of the text on page 7. Which of the words in the box would you expect to see in the article?

> acquaintance
> best friend   boss
> colleague   passer-by
> relationships   roommate
> stranger

b Read the article quickly. Tick (✓) the words in **1a** that appear in the article.

Skills 1

2 Choose the correct option, a, b or c. Then read the text again to check your answers.

1 Robin Dunbar studied
 a how teenagers make friends.
 b some people from very simple societies.
 c the work that people do in modern offices.

2 When they looked at Leila's Facebook friends, they looked at
 a all of her friends.
 b only her closest 50 friends.
 c 50 friends selected by chance.

3 They agreed that someone was a 'real' friend of Leila if
 a they frequently emailed or spoke to her.
 b they had been to school together.
 c they had a lot of acquaintances.

4 They believe that Leila has
 a more real friends than Dunbar's Number.
 b exactly the same number of real friends as Dunbar's Number.
 c fewer real friends than Dunbar's Number.

5 One Facebook friend wasn't Leila's real friend because
 a it was an animal.
 b he was a celebrity.
 c he was a fictional character.

6 Leila's college roommate
 a has dropped out of university.
 b used to get on well with her.
 c meets up with her a lot.

7 The writer concludes that
 a people have more friends because of sites like Facebook.
 b sites like Facebook have no effect at all on our relationships.
 c people use sites like Facebook because they don't like losing past friends.

STRATEGY Before you read a new text, look at the title. This will give you a clue to the content. Then try to think of words or vocabulary that you might expect to see in the article. This can help you understand the content right from the beginning.

How Many Facebook Friends Do We Really Have?

Robin Dunbar of Oxford University believes that the human brain can only remember social groups of up to 150 people. He discovered 'Dunbar's Number' (150) by studying everything from primitive tribes to colleagues in modern offices. But what of the younger generation?

One member of our team, Leila Brillson, has over 500 Facebook friends and she volunteered herself for a small experiment. We wondered if Dunbar's Number would still be true in a Facebook world. What percentage of Leila's virtual friends really were her friends?

The Rules
We chose 50 random friends and then asked Leila questions about them. Depending on the answers, we decided whether the person actually was Leila's friend, based on:
• regular involvement in her life
• strong emotional connection
• continuous effort to stay in touch
If the person didn't meet all of those qualifications, they weren't a friend – just an acquaintance.

The Data
Out of 50 random people, we decided that 31 were not Leila's friends, suggesting that 38% of the people on her Facebook are real friends. 190 friends (38% of 500) isn't far off from Dunbar's 150. Leila knew most of her real friends not through high school but via a social circle, dating or work. Also, anyone that she is a fan of (e.g. a band) is counted by Facebook as a friend, and Leila is certainly not really friends with everyone on her list, like superstar singer Nick Cave.

We argued over three people:

1 College Roommate
Leila insisted that she and her college roommate were still good friends, even though they hadn't seen each other for about four years.

2 Work Colleague
When explaining about a former colleague, Leila mentioned that they ran into each other all the time, and speak every now and again. We decided this was not a friend, but rather a business contact.

3 Ex-best Friend
Despite having grown apart from a good friend in high school, Leila declared they were still friends because of, well, history. We refused this one, because without Facebook, Leila would have no idea where this person was.

Conclusions
Dunbar suggests that there is no 'Facebook effect' -- that social circles do not really expand because of Facebook. What is different though, is that people like Leila have a different definition of a friend to Dunbar. Leila was always hesitant to say someone 'wasn't a friend' -- especially when they once were. Here is the attraction of Facebook: it offers a world where relationships never stop. Sure, old acquaintances may be gone, but now they won't be forgotten.

7

2 EXPERTS

VOCABULARY
Health

1 Circle the word that <u>doesn't</u> work in each sentence.
1. *An acupuncturist / A homeopath / A pharmacist* is an example of an expert in alternative medicine.
2. You need a *chiropractor / herbalist / specialist* to look at your spine.
3. A *herbalist / pharmacist / surgeon* sells cures for various health problems.
4. My dad needed to see a top *acupuncturist / midwife / surgeon* to cure the pain in his neck.
5. My aunt works in the city hospital as a *shaman / nurse / surgeon*.

2 Complete the patient–doctor conversations with the words from the box.

| antibiotics   infection   injection |
| insomnia   rash   vaccination |

1. **P** Can you give me some _____, doctor?
   D No, they won't help you because you have a virus.
2. **P** Why did you want to see us, doctor?
   D All the children in the school are getting a _____ against measles, including your daughter.
3. **D** I'm sorry, but I have to give you an _____.
   P Oh no! Will it be painful?
4. **P** I'm not sleeping well at the moment. I feel exhausted all the time!
   D I'm sorry to hear that. I expect you have _____.
5. **P** I cut my foot and then I went swimming and now look at it. The cut won't heal!
   D Every time you cut yourself, you should wash the cut and cover it, to prevent _____.
6. **P** I started using this medicine and now I have a _____ on my arm – look! All my skin is red.
   D Right, I think we should change that medicine.

3 Complete the words.
1. You get b _ _ ka _ _ e because you sit badly at your desk.
2. The most popular p _ _ nk _ l _ _ _ _ s are aspirin and paracetamol.
3. The surgeons performed a seven-hour heart o _ e _ a _ _ o _ .
4. I fell off my bike and now I have a big black b _ _ _ s _ on my elbow.
5. Can you buy me some cough m _ x _ _ _ _ e if you go to the chemist's?
6. Oh dear, your forehead feels very hot. I think you might have a hight t _ _ p _ _ at _ _ _ _ .
7. I was hit by a golf ball and now I have a l _ _ p on my head!

4 Choose the correct options to complete the sentences.
1. Have you *taken / done* your medicine yet?
2. You need to *make / do* an appointment with the doctor.
3. I think you have a fever. I'll *make / take* your temperature.
4. The doctor will *write / do* you a prescription.
5. Gina's gone to bed because she *did / felt* sick.
6. We can *take / treat* this illness with antibiotics.
7. Fatima's not well. She *got / took* an infection at the weekend.
8. Oh dear, you *feel / have* all the symptoms of flu.

Medicine

5 Complete the text with the words from the box.

| bandage   medication   nurses   paramedic |
| patients   surgeons   theatre   wards |

I love my job because…

So what do you do, Lindsay?
I'm a (1)_____ – I work with the ambulance team at the local hospital.

And is it a difficult job?
That depends. It can be very stressful. Sometimes our work is just putting a (2)_____ on a person's injury, or giving them some (3)_____ . At other times, we have to get someone to an operating (4)_____ as quickly as possible, for example after an accident. It can be a matter of life and death.

Of course. Do you spend time at the hospital, too?
I rarely spend time on the hospital (5)_____ , unless I am visiting someone we've helped. When we get to the hospital, our job is done. After that, we have to leave the (6)_____ and other specialists to do what they can.

And what's the best thing about your job?
The people. I feel that I can make a difference to the lives of our (7)_____ , which means a lot to me. The doctors and (8)_____ at the hospital are great, too. I wouldn't change my job for anything in the world!

8

6 Complete the *-ever* words.

1 A You failed your driving test again. Are you going to stop taking lessons?
  B No! I am going to learn to drive _____ever many lessons it takes me!

2 A Is it OK if I sit here?
  B Yes, sit _____ever you like. Make yourself at home.

3 A _____ever you do, don't tell Jim about the party!
  B Don't worry, I won't tell him anything.

4 A I feel terrible! I don't know if it's flu, or just a cold.
  B Well, I don't think you can go to work today _____ever you have.

5 A I'm asking all the teachers if they want to go on the school trip next Saturday.
  B Well, _____ever decides to go needs to know about first aid.

6 A What time should I come to your house on Saturday?
  B You can come _____ever you like. We'll be in all day.

VOCABULARY EXTENSION
Treatment

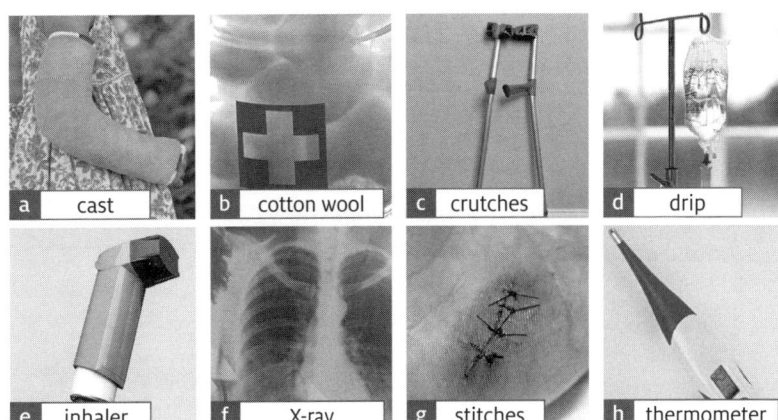

a cast   b cotton wool   c crutches   d drip
e inhaler   f X-ray   g stitches   h thermometer

7 Complete the sentences with the words from the photos.

1 Dana got hurt playing hockey and she needed six _____ in her forehead.
2 You're not allowed to drink anything before the operation, so we're going to put you on a _____ .
3 The surgeon isn't sure what's wrong with your toe, so she wants to do an _____ of your foot.
4 I have asthma, but it's OK. I just use my _____ when I'm having breathing difficulties.
5 Use this _____ to take your temperature.
6 Rosie has broken her arm and it's in a _____ – all her friends have written messages on it!
7 I can't walk without _____ . My legs hurt too much.
8 The nurse will get some _____ to clean the blood on your knee.

BRING IT TOGETHER

8 Complete the text with the words from the box. There are two words that you don't need.

appointment backache diagnosis however patient
plaster prescription treat whatever whenever

Acupuncture

Acupuncture began in ancient China where it was used to (1)_____ a huge number of illnesses and diseases. Today it remains popular, although many doctors only recommend it for certain problems like (2)_____ .

So how does it work? Once you make an (3)_____ with the acupuncturist, he or she will try to find out all about your health. Then the acupuncturist will ask the (4)_____ to lie down to begin the treatment. During a visit he/she may insert up to a dozen metal needles.

Acupuncture is a form of alternative medicine. So if you choose to try it, (5)_____ you do, do not stop taking other medicines. If you have a (6)_____ from your normal doctor, continue using it.

It is also best to get a clear (7)_____ of your problem from a normal doctor. In some countries (like England) anyone can be an acupuncturist. So (8)_____ you go to see one, make sure that they have proper qualifications from a professional organisation.

2

GRAMMAR
The present

1 Choose the correct options to complete the sentences.

1 The pharmacy *opens / is opening* at 8.30 a.m.
2 *I really hate / I'm really hating* injections. I'm scared of needles!
3 My father *is taking / takes* medication every day.
4 My nursing course *starts / is starting* next month.
5 *I often get / I'm often getting* colds in winter.
6 Jan *is taking / takes* antibiotics at the moment. He has an infection.
7 *I go / I'm going* to the pharmacy now to get my dad's prescription.
8 The surgeon *waits / is waiting* in the operating theatre.

2 Match a–b to i–ii.

1 a My sister goes ____
   b They're going ____
   i   running in the park.
   ii running every day.

2 a I'm thinking ____
   b I think ____
   i   about joining a gym.
   ii gyms are a waste of money.

3 a This bruise feels ____
   b You're feeling ____
   i   well again.
   ii really painful.

4 a He's always hated ____
   b He's hating ____
   i   going to the doctor.
   ii his medicine course.

5 a I'm always taking painkillers ____
   b I always take painkillers ____
   i   because I have a bad back.
   ii when I have backache.

6 a He's trying ____
   b He has tried ____
   i   taking diet pills.
   ii to lose weight at the moment.

7 a I've done yoga ____
   b I do yoga ____
   i   because it helps me relax.
   ii since I was young.

3 Complete the text with the correct form of the verbs in brackets.

Pilates Blog

I'm Lola Puyol and I'm a Pilates instructor in Caracas. Welcome to my first ever blog! I (1)_____ (write) it to tell people about Pilates and my life.

So what is Pilates? It's a way of keeping in shape. Millions of people (2)_____ (do) it worldwide every day. It (3)_____ (strengthen) your mind and body. Pilates students also (4)_____ (use) a lot of equipment. For example, in the picture, I (5)_____ (teach) one of my students how to use 'the reformer'. Alba, my student, (6)_____ (push) with her legs to build up the core muscles of the body. This is probably our most famous piece of equipment.

As for me, I (7)_____ (be) a teacher of Pilates for eight years now, but there are still things I want to learn. For the next seven days, my friend Antonio and I (8)_____ (take) a course to become better teachers. It was Antonio's idea. He (9)_____ (think) that we should do it to improve our knowledge of all the techniques.

Pilates isn't just for fun, either. Some American scientists (10)_____ (study) Pilates at the moment to see if it can help patients with Parkinson's Disease. I'll tell you more about that next week.

Comments 0   posted Tuesday March 29, 11.13 a.m.

4 Correct the sentences. Tick (✓) two correct sentences.

1 I'm being a pharmacist for almost 20 years.
2 I'm not believing in alternative medicine.
3 Do you take any medicine at the moment?
4 Jean's going to the chiropractor every fortnight.
5 You are needing a vaccination before you go on holiday.
6 Chris has felt ill all week.
7 You're always catching colds!
8 I try to lose weight at the moment.

Used to do/used to doing

5 a Put the words in the correct order to make sentences.

1 used   pills   she   to   take   diet
_____

2 not   I'm   doing   to   exercise   used
_____

3 to   use   a   personal   didn't   we   have   trainer
_____

4 taking   medicine   he's   used   to   the   getting
_____

5 in   to   can't   used   I   get   hospital   being
_____

b Which sentences in **5a** describe
i   the past?   _____
ii the present? _____

6 Complete the sentences with one word in each gap (*don't*, etc. = one word).

> When I was younger, I ⁽¹⁾_____ to be really unfit. I didn't ⁽²⁾_____ to like walking – I drove everywhere! I felt tired all the time and I ⁽³⁾_____ to get a lot of headaches, but I didn't think there was anything wrong. I was ⁽⁴⁾_____ to feeling like that. Then my partner encouraged me to start exercising and, within just a few weeks, the headaches were gone!
> Now I'm much more healthy. I go running about three mornings a week. At first I didn't enjoy getting up early, but I ⁽⁵⁾_____ used to it now – it's part of my routine. I'm also ⁽⁶⁾_____ used to eating a healthier diet. I ⁽⁷⁾_____ to buy a lot of ready meals, but now I cook more fresh food. I still don't like vegetables much, but I think I'll ⁽⁸⁾_____ used to them eventually!

7 Complete the sentences with the correct form of the words in brackets and the correct form of *used to*.

1 _____ (you/eat) a lot of junk food when you were young?
2 Nikos still doesn't like the gym, but now he has a personal trainer, he _____ (go) there.
3 I'm not used to having backache – I _____ (not/get) it when I was younger.
4 My grandma _____ (take) an aspirin every day. She's done it for years.
5 Lots of people find acupuncture strange at first, but they quickly _____ (have) the treatment.
6 I'm a paediatrician so I _____ (not/working) with adults – I only treat children.

BRING IT TOGETHER

8 Choose the correct options to complete the messages from an advice website.

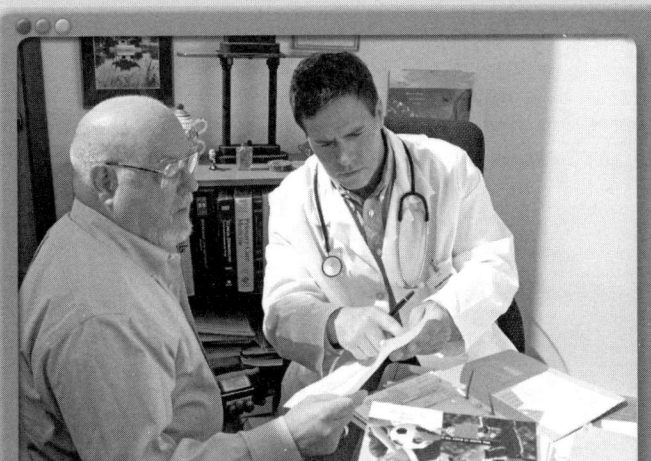

Self-diagnosis?

At the moment, my partner ⁽¹⁾*suffers / is suffering* from a red rash on his leg. ⁽²⁾*He has / He's had* the symptoms for a week now and they don't seem to be getting better. Today he ⁽³⁾*reads / is reading* about his symptoms online and now he wants to do some self-medication! I'm worried because, in this country, pharmacists ⁽⁴⁾*sell / are selling* many medicines without a prescription – including powerful drugs like antibiotics! What can I do?

AG

This isn't a new problem. Before modern hospitals, people ⁽⁵⁾*use to / used to* invent their own cures for diseases – but that didn't mean the cures worked. Today, many people ⁽⁶⁾*are / get* used to looking at the internet when they feel ill. This is harmless if they look at websites by medical professionals. However, it cannot replace a visit to the doctor. Many people ⁽⁷⁾*don't understand / aren't understanding* that certain symptoms have different causes. The last time I heard about someone with this problem, I advised her to bring her printouts to the surgery. That patient ⁽⁸⁾*has now been / has now got* used to doing this and discusses the possible symptoms with her doctor. Maybe the same system could work for your partner, too?

MD

Skills development

Functional language
Making polite requests

1 🔊 2.1 Listen to a conversation in a doctor's surgery. Complete the appointment card.

```
Patient name: Jennifer Chan
Appointment with: _____
Date: _____
Time: _____
```

2 a Complete the questions from the conversation in **1**.
1 I _____ if you _____ give me some advice?
2 _____ you _____ me if I need any vaccinations?
3 Would it be _____ to get the vaccinations in the surgery?
4 Do you _____ any _____ how long the appointment will take?
5 _____ you _____ writing that on a card for me?

b Listen again and check.

Listening Choosing the correct option

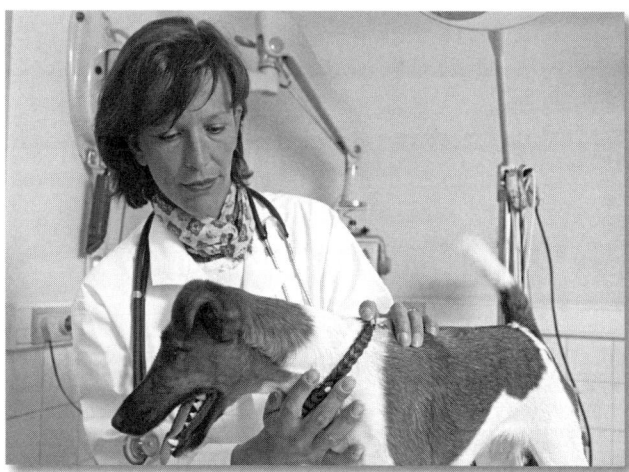

1 🔊 2.2 Listen to a radio programme about training to become a vet. Number topics a–e in the order you hear about them.
a work experience   _____
b disadvantages of being a vet   _____
c types of animal   _____
d school subjects   _____
e advice about university   _____

2 a Choose the correct answers to the questions.
1 What kind of animals does Alexandra work with now?
  a farm animals
  b family pets
  c unusual animals
2 Which school subject is Gemma best at?
  a Biology
  b Chemistry
  c Maths
3 Where is Gemma working as a volunteer?
  a at an animal shelter
  b at a local farm
  c at a riding centre
4 What warning does Alexandra give about working as a vet?
  a Vets get badly injured by the animals they work with.
  b Vets have to make difficult decisions.
  c Vets must work very long hours.
5 What should Gemma do before beginning university?
  a go travelling
  b get advice about finances
  c do a lot of studying

b Listen again and check.

> **Strategy** When you have to answer multiple-choice questions, read the questions and options carefully. Remember that all the options may contain words from the audio. The first time you listen, try to identify the correct answers. The second time you listen, check your answers. Why are the other options wrong?

Skills 2

Writing Using facts & figures

1 Read the blog post quickly and answer the questions.
1 What type of images are A–C?
2 Which countries do the data in A–C come from?

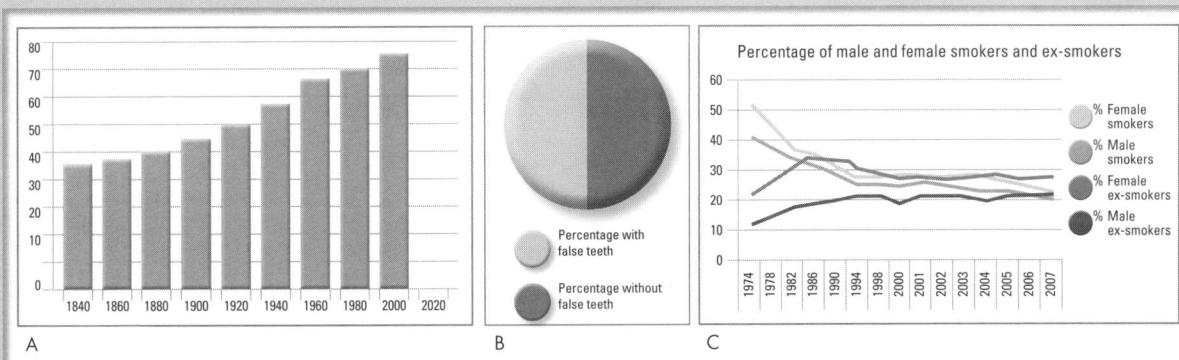

The good old days? – Rutger Van Sciver

This week there has been a whole series of TV programmes about declining health in society. I disagree with them so strongly that I had to write about it. The good old days never happened! I'm going to look at some statistics from three different countries, but I think they show general trends. All of these diagrams were sourced from the internet.

First of all, if people were healthier in the past, why was life expectancy so low? Look at figure A, the bar chart for the USA. This reveals that in 1920, most people died before they were 50. A century ago, most people never met their grandparents. It can clearly be seen that life expectancy has risen year on year, even during depressions and wars.

People don't just live longer, they live better too. Take diagram B, the pie chart from my country, the Netherlands. It tells us that back in 1981, roughly half of all people had false teeth. People didn't look after themselves in the same way in the past, and things like toothpaste, mouthwash and dental floss were nowhere near as good as they are today. Nowadays the percentage of people with false teeth is less than 33%.

This brings me to my third visual, chart C. What this line graph demonstrates is that the number of smokers in the UK has fallen every year since 1974. This has an overall impact on the entire population. I was born in 1960 and I can remember in my childhood that cigarette smoke was everywhere – on buses, in cinemas and even on planes. Now this has completely changed: it's another example of how people today take better care of their health. We live longer, cleaner and healthier lives. So how can people say that things were better in the past?

2 Complete the sentences with the missing words. Check your answers in the blog post.
1 I'm going to look at some st _ _ _ s _ _ cs from three different countries, but I think they s _ _ _ general trends.
2 All of these diagrams were s _ _ _ c _ d from the internet.
3 Look at f _ g _ _ _ A, the bar chart for the USA. This r _ v _ _ _ s that…
4 It can c _ _ _ _ r _ y be seen that life expectancy has r _ _ _ n year on year.
5 Take d _ _ g _ _ m B, the pie chart from my country, the Netherlands. It t _ _ _ s us that back in 1981, over half of all people had false teeth.
6 Nowadays the p _ _ cent _ _ _ of people with false teeth is less than 33%.
7 What this line graph d _ m _ _ _ s _ r _ t _ s is that…

3 Write a reply to Rutger's blog post. Do you agree or disagree with his argument? Refer to his diagrams or any others that you can find online.

Strategy

When we refer to charts or diagrams, we usually use the present simple tense and verbs like *reveal, show, tell*. We use the noun form to describe the data that they show e.g. *the number of smokers, the percentage of people*. Notice that we say data is *in* the chart or *in* the diagram.

3 SURVIVAL

VOCABULARY
Equipment

1 a Complete the text with the words from the box.

> compasses   life jackets   life rafts   rope
> sails   waterproof clothing

It's one thing to travel across the ocean in a boat with ⁽¹⁾ _____ for wind power – but how about crossing the Pacific using only the strength of your arms? Turkey's Erden Eruç set out to do just that in 2007.

An ocean crossing is incredibly dangerous and Eruç was careful to keep safe. On board, he had plenty of ⁽²⁾ _____ to keep him dry, and he also had space for two ⁽³⁾ _____ to replace his main boat if it sank! Eruç took two ⁽⁴⁾ _____ to find North, and two ⁽⁵⁾ _____ to wear if he got thrown out of the boat. Falling into the ocean would be really dangerous, so he also had a ⁽⁶⁾ _____ tying his leg to the boat.

Unfortunately, even with these preparations, Eruç had to abandon his trip in May 2008 when the crossing became impossible. But in 2010, Eruç finally achieved his dream and in doing so he became the first person to have rowed across three oceans – the Atlantic, the Indian and the Pacific.

b Match 1–6 to a–f.

1 Is that a boat over there? I can't see very well. ___
2 That's a bad cut on your leg. ___
3 We don't need a map. ___
4 There's no electricity and it's really dark. ___
5 Don't forget to pack your thermal underwear! ___
6 Radar is very useful if you have to navigate in poor weather. ___

a There's a GPS in the car.
b You can use it to see where other boats are.
c Pass me the binoculars, please.
d Do you know where the torch is?
e That will keep you warm when you're in Canada.
f It's lucky there's a first aid box.

Personality adjectives

2 Complete the words.

1 You have to be very d__t__ m__n__d to complete a marathon. It's a lot of hard work.
2 Vicky is very m__tu__ for her age. She's 14, but she acts like an 18-year-old.
3 Our team is w__ l-p__ p__ ed for the expedition. We have bought all the equipment we need.
4 I think hikers who leave rubbish in the natural park are completely ir__ __ p__ __ ib__ __.
5 After the earthquake, many people were saved by the c__ r__ ge__ __ actions of firefighters, who were working in very dangerous conditions.
6 Carl is r__ k__ ss because he takes so many unnecessary risks.
7 Shin-cho is a very ex__ __ ie__ __ __ mountain climber. He's been to the Alps, the Andes and the Himalayas.
8 Dino is a very r__ s__ l__ nt tennis player. He very often has a difficult match, but wins it in the end.
9 The boat has everything we need to survive at sea. We can be completely s__ l__ -s__ ff__ __ __ n__.
10 To drive across the desert, you need to be very r__ s__ u__ c__ f__ l. There will lots of problems, and you can't predict them.

Talking about danger

3 Correct the sentences. Tick (✓) two correct sentences.

1 If you don't take a compass, you're at danger of getting lost.
2 We got into trouble while we were kayaking and we had to call for help.
3 My friends go diving, but I just watch them in safe from the boat!
4 Don't do risks when you're swimming in the sea. Anything can happen.
5 Everything got wrong on the holiday: the flight was delayed, the kids got sick and the hotel was terrible.
6 I'm going to go backpacking round the world. I'm not care about the risks!
7 Our travel agency will take all the necessary precautions before we go white-water rafting.
8 We need to warn the tourists on pickpockets on the trains.

Weather

4 Read the clues and complete the puzzle. What is the hidden word in grey? _____

1 Bursts of very bright light that you see in a storm.
2 A thick cloud at ground level that makes it very difficult to see.
3 Strong winds and a lot of snowfall.
4 A loud noise you hear during a bad storm.
5 A very strong (e.g. 100 kilometre-per-hour) wind.
6 A pile of deep snow created by the wind.
7 Small balls of ice that fall from the sky.

Vocabulary extension
Word building

5 Complete the word chart.

Verb	Noun	Adjective
(1)	(2)	(un)assisted
damage	(3)	(4)
isolate	(5)	(6)
injure	(7)	injured
recognise	(8)	(9) (un)
(10)	rescue / rescuer	
	severity	(11)
survive	(12) survival /	

6 a Complete the sentences with the correct form of six words from **5**.

1 After the tornado, the emergency services soon started searching for _____ .
2 The storm caused a lot of _____ to her boat, but she was able to sail to safety.
3 They managed to get out of the snowdrift with a bit of _____ .
4 We feel quite _____ in the winter – the snow makes it hard for people to visit us.
5 It was a _____ storm, which affected large areas of the country.
6 His car was so badly damaged that it was _____ .

b 🔊 3.1 Listen and check.

Bring it together

7 Complete the text with the words from the box.

> blizzard   precautions   radar   reckless
> rescue   risks   snowdrifts   survival
> waterproof clothing   well-prepared

> **avalanche** *(n)* /ˈævəlɑːntʃ/
> a sudden fall of snow from a mountainside

Safety in the mountains

If you enjoy winter sports in the mountains you need to be aware of the (1)_____ involved so that you stay safe. If you are caught in a storm, you need to be wearing (2)_____ so that you stay dry. It is a good idea to wear goggles too. These can help if you are caught in a (3)_____ ; without them, you can be blinded by the snow. Poles are useful too as bad weather can produce (4)_____ , where snow is blown into a pile by the wind.

It is also important to be aware of the danger of avalanches. You need to check the weather conditions and find out about the terrain you are planning to cross. You also need to make sure you are (5)_____ . For example, you should carry a device called an ARVA. This will enable others to (6)_____ you if you are caught by an avalanche and buried under snow. Some people also use a gadget that uses (7)_____ , like on ships. In an avalanche, you have a 50% chance of death if you are buried for more than 20 minutes, so not carrying these devices is incredibly (8)_____ . Your chances of (9)_____ may depend on you and others in your party having one, so they are essential pieces of equipment.

You can enjoy doing winter sports in safety – if you take sensible (10)_____ before you go into the mountains and while you are there.

3

GRAMMAR
Narrative tenses

1 Complete the sentences with one word in each gap (*don't*, etc. = one word).

1 There was a bad storm yesterday so we _____ go sailing.
2 What _____ you doing when the storm started?
3 They _____ heard the news before I called them. It was a shock for them!
4 He was exhausted because he'd _____ climbing all day.
5 When the boat began to sink, many passengers jumped into the water and _____ to the shore.
6 We were very tired because we _____ been walking in the snow for hours.
7 Last night, Cathy _____ steering the boat while I _____ sleeping.
8 _____ anyone checked the weather forecast before you started the expedition?

2 Choose the correct options to complete the sentences.

1 When I looked through the binoculars, I *saw / was seeing* the island.
2 When they were rescued, they *had spent / were spending* three weeks underground.
3 Mum called us while we *had travelled / were travelling* on the train.
4 They were incredibly relieved to see another ship. They *sat / had been sitting* in the life raft for three days.
5 I didn't want to disturb Don because he *studied / was studying* the map.
6 When we were at sea, we realised we *hadn't packed / weren't packing* the first aid box.
7 The forest fire *had burnt / had been burning* for two hours before the firefighters arrived to put it out.
8 They checked the life rafts. They *set / were setting* the GPS, and then they left.
9 After I got into the dive cage, I realised that I *hadn't charged / had been charging* my camera battery.
10 We arrived at the airport just as check-in *was closing / had been closing*, so we were able to get on the plane.

3 Use the words to write sentences in the past.

1 I feel tired because I run
   I felt tired because I had been running.
2 Rita meet her boyfriend when they travel on a bus
   _____
3 Elena not go rock climbing last weekend because she hurt her arm
   _____
4 the girls see an eagle when they camp in the woods
   _____
5 we need a break because we drive for hours
   _____
6 while Alfonso drive to his girlfriend's house a hailstorm suddenly start
   _____

4 Complete the text with the past continuous, past perfect or past perfect continuous form of the verbs in brackets.

Shipwrecked on Mogmog

The island of Mogmog is one of the most remote places on Earth, and for the next six months it will be home to the Barrie family from Australia. Last month, the Barries [1]_____ (sail) across the Pacific when they were caught in a storm. While hurricane-force winds [2]_____ (blow) across their boat, they decided to head for the safety of Mogmog. Unfortunately, their boat was damaged when it [3]_____ (approach) the beach. It hit some metal that American soldiers [4]_____ (leave) there 60 years ago. Fortunately, the islanders helped them bring the boat ashore, although one man injured his hand when they [5]_____ (take) it out of the water.

Although the family were delighted to be safe, they soon realised their boat needed serious repairs. After Mr Barrie [6]_____ (speak) to experts back home, he discovered that they needed six months to complete them. Fortunately, the islanders have made their guests very welcome. The Barries' daughters were especially pleased to meet the local children after they [7]_____ (spend) months at sea. Now they spend their time playing on the beach – but it's not all fun in the sun. Before the accident, they [8]_____ (study) online with a teacher in Australia and once they arrived on Mogmog, their lessons started again!

Adverbs

5 a Complete the sentences with the adverb form of the word in brackets.
1. *Happily,* everything went well at the party. (happy)
2. He goes rock climbing at the weekend. (usual)
3. It was hot on the coach. (uncomfortable)
4. There was a snowstorm so we couldn't go climbing. (unfortunate)
5. I am asked why I love taking risks. (frequent)
6. She speaks French. (good)
7. The hotel was cheap. (reasonable)
8. I studied the route before I set off. (careful)
9. Thrill seekers find activities like white-water rafting exciting. (extreme)
10. I don't like taking risks. (person)

b Complete the chart with the adverbs in **5a**.

Adverb of manner	Adverb of frequency	Adverb to modify an adjective	Sentence adverb
			happily

6 Put the words in the correct order to make sentences.
1. skilfully   climbed   she   mountain   the
2. hardly   risks   takes   he   ever
3. discuss   carefully   this   to   need   you
4. in   their   danger   want   lives   people   often   some
5. the   ill   surprisingly   voyage   nobody   on   got
6. is   highly   he   sailor   experienced   a

7 Correct the sentences. Tick (✓) three correct sentences.
1. Extreme sports are gradually becoming more expensive.
2. We take usually all the necessary precautions.
3. She's a thrill seeker so always she's trying new activities.
4. My sailing teacher speaks very quickly!
5. Diving with sharks is dangerous extremely.
6. Interestingly, the first bungee jump happened on Vanuatu, a Pacific island.
7. I go sometimes rock climbing at the sports centre.
8. My boyfriend can read very well maps.

BRING IT TOGETHER

8 Choose the correct options to complete the text.

This year's weirdest weather

Onlookers were astonished to see lightning during the eruption of Mount Shinmoedake in January. Whilst people ⁽¹⁾*had watched / were watching* the eruption of the Japanese volcano, strange lights appeared in the sky above it. Local people ⁽²⁾*had never seen / never had seen* anything like it before, which was not surprising as experts ⁽³⁾*are still not / are not still* exactly certain why it occurred.

Planes were left waiting at Lagos airport in October as a mysterious fog appeared in Nigeria. The fog covered everything with white dust so many people ⁽⁴⁾*had walked / were walking* around with grey hair and clothes. By the time it finally ended, some towns ⁽⁵⁾*hadn't seen / weren't seeing* the sun for four days. Afterwards, local experts explained that the dust ⁽⁶⁾*had blown / was blowing* into the country from the Sahara to create the strange effect.

At the end of the year, a sudden storm hit Perth, Australia. Three centimetres of rain fell in just 15 minutes and several buildings collapsed after the rain ⁽⁷⁾*had damaged / was damaging* their roofs. While the floodwaters ⁽⁸⁾*had risen / were rising*, many people decided to leave their houses. Most people ⁽⁹⁾*left calmly their homes / left their homes calmly* without any signs of panic, once again showing how ⁽¹⁰⁾*resilient amazingly / amazingly resilient* the Australian people are in the face of disaster.

Skills development

Functional language
Giving warnings

1 Complete the words.

Hi Mick

I can't believe that you're going on safari! In your email, you asked me for some advice. Here it is!

(1)R_____ to get full medical insurance because you'll come into contact with wild animals. It's also important to see the doctor to get vaccinations before you leave. You definitely (2)s_____ forget to take anti-malaria tablets, either. Malaria's a real problem in some areas so you want to be (3)c_____ if you're going to be in any of them. You (4)m_____ want to take a mosquito net too to give you extra protection.

Make (5)s_____ you take an adapter, to recharge your camera or your mobile. Speaking of photography, you should buy extra memory cards because you'll take so many pictures. You (6)m_____ also want to pack sun cream. I (7)w_____ buy that sort of thing while you're overseas because it's cheaper at home. You could also buy a guide to the birds of Africa because you'll see lots and it's impossible to remember their names.

Otherwise, you (8)d_____ want to worry too much. It's going to be a lot of fun!

Bye for now

Joseph

Listening
Listening for specific information

1 a 🔊 3.2 You are going to listen to the weather forecast for South Africa. Listen and number the places in the order you hear them.

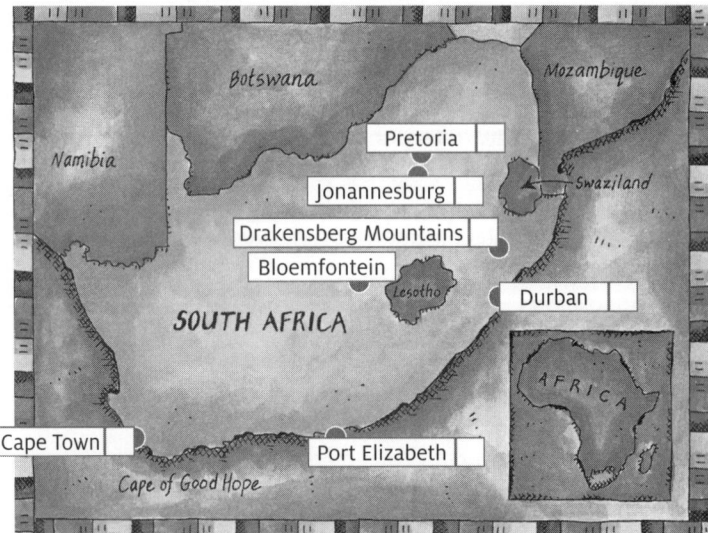

b How many severe weather warnings did you hear? Where were they for? _____

2 a Read the weather forecast summary. In which gap(s) is/are the missing word(s)

a a number? _____
b a noun? _____
c an adjective? _____
d an adverb? _____

Cape Town	(1)_____ in the early morning – remember to drive (2)_____!
Durban	clear (3)_____ and (4)_____ weather throughout the day.
Pretoria	maximum temperature of (5)_____°C. There is a possibility of (6)_____ mid-afternoon.
Drakensberg Mountains	risk of (7)_____ and large (8)_____ in some areas.

b Listen again. Complete the summary with one word in each gap.

> **Strategy** Before you listen, read the questions carefully and decide what kind of information you need to listen for. Remember, you don't need to understand every word you hear!

Skills 3

Reading Referencing devices

1 a Read the text. Match sentences a–g to gaps 1–6. There is one sentence that you do not need.

a The next step is the hardest, and will test how resilient the six men really are.
b There were more than 100 experiments programmed.
c One from Colombia, France and China with the others all from Russia.
d They hadn't even left the Earth's atmosphere.
e Their only contact with the outside world was via the internet.
f For example, what is the effect of radiation on travellers in deep space?
g Then they made a hole in the planet surface to take rock and dust samples.

b Read the text again. Then look at the Strategy box. Underline examples of the three patterns in the text

2 Answer the questions.

1 What did the men take to place on the surface of 'Mars'?

2 How long was the mission?

3 Why was communication not instant?

4 What other name is given for Mars in the text?

5 What institution helped the men to prepare?

6 How did the astronauts practise their medical skills?

> **Strategy** To help you understand a long text, look out for patterns that show you how ideas connect together. These might be
> - a series of phrases (e.g. *firstly, then, next*)
> - linking phrases that connect one idea to another (e.g. *however, actually, for example*)
> - or words that replace an earlier idea in the text (e.g. *this, that, these*).

Mission to Mars

On Monday, 14 February 2011, human beings finally walked across the surface of Mars. First, they investigated the local terrain. (1)_____ After leaving three flags representing the international crew – from China, Russia and Europe – the courageous explorers returned to the safety of the their spacecraft, Mars500... except that it didn't happen quite like that.

In fact, the three men were walking along the floor of a building in Russia. They hadn't travelled through space. (2)_____ They were taking part in the Mars500 project, a simulation to see how human beings react on a long journey through space.

We are not at the stage of a manned mission to Mars yet because there are still a lot of unanswered questions. (3)_____ We don't know yet. Before they can take the risk of sending a spacecraft across the solar system, scientists also need to know how six people react to living in such a small area for over a year and a half.

To do this, they developed the Mars500 project, where six volunteers agreed to spend 519 days in a space ship, separated from the outside world – and pretending to go through space. (4)_____ However, even that had a 20 minute delay to represent the time it takes messages to travel across space from Earth.

Before their arrival on the red planet, the men had been performing a series of tasks to see how resourceful they needed to be. (5)_____ These included performing mock operations, as there would be no access to surgeons or other experts during the trip. Thankfully, they were well-prepared because they had spent months practising with the staff of Mainz University before the trip began, and they performed their operation (on a model – not a real person!) without any major errors.

(6)_____ They must turn around and return to Earth, facing another difficult 240 days on board. Then finally they can meet their waiting families and tell them their stories of the year and a half that they spent travelling... nowhere.

PROGRESS TEST 1

GRAMMAR & VOCABULARY
(25 points)

1 Rewrite the sentences using the word in bold. Do not change the word given. (*10 points*)

0 Kostas is your line manager – is that correct?
   Kostas is your line manager, isn't he?   **isn't**

1 Who was this blog written by?
   _____   **wrote**

2 The optician tested my eyes.
   _____   **had**

3 It's not normal for me to get up at 6 a.m.
   _____   **used**

4 I started working here five years ago.
   _____   **have**

5 I was waiting for an hour before the bus arrived.
   _____   **been**

2 Complete the sentences with the words from the box. (*8 points*)

| acupuncturist | antibiotics | binoculars | bruise |
| fog | gale | ~~partner~~ | passenger | raft |

0 I live with Rachel, but we're not married – she's my *partner*.
1 I want to see what's on the mountaintop. Pass me the _____.
2 Tomas has a bad _____ on his arm – it's gone purple!
3 It was difficult to drive because of the thick _____.
4 Several trees were blown down during the _____.
5 There was no one on the train but me. I was the only _____.
6 After she visited the _____, my grandmother's back pain disappeared.
7 We have a life _____ in case there's an accident on board the ship.
8 Luckily, we can treat a bacterial infection with _____.

3 Match 1–7 to a–h. (*7 points*)

0 Bad news. Sharon and her boyfriend have split   *d*
1 Frank and Hans are good friends. They really get _____
2 If you want Rick to be your boyfriend, you have to ask him _____
3 The nurse asked to take my _____
4 The surgeon can't see you because she's working in the operating _____
5 A lifeguard had to rescue me at the beach after I got into _____
6 I have some bad news for you. Something has gone badly _____
7 You can only get this medicine if the doctor writes you a _____

a out.   b theatre.   c wrong.   ~~d up.~~
e trouble.   f prescription. g on.   h temperature.

READING (25 points)

1 Choose the best title for the text. (*3 points*)

1 The death of the guidebook
2 Guidebooks go online
3 Why I still use guidebooks

2 Complete gaps 1–6 in the text with missing sentences a–g. (*12 points*)

a What's more, reviewers usually say something about themselves.
b With a few quick tweets, you can find the latest restaurants, hotels and places to see.
c It's voice-activated.
d He was a complete snob!
e Well… no, not anymore.
f That person might give a place a good review just because the owners were nice to him/her.
g Plane tickets? Passport? Travel insurance?

Sun cream? Check! Mobile phone? Check! (0) _g_ Check! Check! Check! Guidebook? (1)_____ People just don't want them these days. Like many other reference works like dictionaries, encyclopedias and atlases, the day of the guidebook might be over. It's all the fault of the World Wide Web.

While carrying our tablets and laptops, we can get much more information more quickly over the internet. Twitter is one of the best means of getting top tips for your next travel location. (2)_____ People will also tell you the places that are closest to you.

If it's reviews you're after, what guidebook could match websites like Trip Advisor? In your guidebook, you get just one person's opinion of a hotel. (3)_____ And of course, as soon as a place is mentioned in a famous guide, room prices go up overnight. That cheap stay has just become one of the most expensive beds in the city!

Even the people selling the trips are getting involved. On Booking.com you can read reviews from a range of users. (4)_____ This is a real advantage, because we all have different needs when we travel. With peer reviews, you can see whether a hotel is good for people like you. When you read a guidebook, on the other hand, you hope that the author thinks like you, but that's not always the case. I once went on a trip to Brazil with a guidebook and I really disagreed with the author. (5)_____ If a beach wasn't totally isolated, miles and miles from the nearest house, he hated it! Personally, I quite like to sunbathe on a beach near my hotel.

The truly amazing thing is that the internet is changing incredibly quickly. Over in the USA, they've just started using an iPhone app called Siri. (6)_____ You talk into it, and it processes all the information on the web to get the best travel information. However, it only works in the States at the moment. So, goodbye guidebook authors – we're all experts now!

TEST 1

3 Answer the questions. (*10 points*)

1 What other books does the author mention in the article, apart from guidebooks?
  _____
2 Which website is useful if you don't want to walk a long way from your present location? Why?
  _____
3 What happens when a hotel appears in a guidebook?
  _____
4 Why did the author of the article disagree with a guidebook author?
  _____
5 Why is Siri not yet good for someone travelling around the world?
  _____

LISTENING (*25 points*)

1 🔊 T1 Listen to five short conversations. Where are the people? (*5 points*)

Conversation 1 _____
Conversation 2 _____
Conversation 3 _____
Conversation 4 _____
Conversation 5 _____

2 Listen again. Match the speakers to the relationships. There is one answer that you don't need. (*10 points*)

In which conversation (1–5), are the speakers

a in-laws? _____
b a stranger and a passer-by? _____
c acquaintances? _____
d team-mates? _____
e colleagues? _____
f husband and wife? _____

3 Choose the correct options. (*10 points*)

1 In conversation 1, what does Barry want for his sailing trip?
  a Some clothing.
  b Some medical equipment.
  c Some technology.
2 In conversation 2, What is Janet's job?
  a A homeopath.   b A midwife.   c A surgeon.
3 In conversation 3, why is Lee not feeling well?
  a Because of something he ate.
  b Because of the hot weather.
  c Because of an injection.
4 In conversation 4, what is the family going to do?
  a Go on some rides.
  b Visit the zoo.
  c Walk around a museum.
5 In conversation 5, why were Harry and Pamela successful?
  a They're really determined.
  b They're really experienced.
  c They're really reckless.

WRITING (*25 points*)

1 Complete the blog post with one word in each gap. Do you agree with the advice? (*5 points*)

> Help! I'm 16 and I really want to go on an ice-climbing trip with my friends. The problem is that my parents think it's too dangerous and they don't want me to go. What should I do?
>
> Jess
>
> Hi Jess
> This is a difficult one. The first thing (o) _is_ to ensure that your ice-climbing trip is being organised by professionals. You (1) _____ overestimate how important this is. The mountains are dangerous, and you need to know your instructor is qualified to deal with emergencies. Whatever you (2) _____ , don't go with an unqualified group leader.
> After you have checked this, my advice (3) _____ be to do lots of research on ice-climbing that you can give to your parents. It's important (4) _____ show them that ice-climbing is pretty safe if you do it the right way. If I (5) _____ you, I'd also contact the organisers of the ice-climbing trip and ask them to talk to your family. That way, your parents will feel better about the trip, and perhaps they'll change their minds.
> Good luck!
>
> Xenia

2 Read the blog post. Write a reply to Felipe, giving him some advice. (*20 points*)

> Hi everyone,
> My son's 18 and he's just heard that he has to go into hospital for an operation on his leg. It's really bad news because he wanted to start university next month, but now he has to wait until next year. He's feeling really depressed and frustrated because all his friends are going away to study, but he has to spend two months in a hospital ward. What can I do to make him feel better? Do you have any ideas? He loves learning languages and travelling.
> Thanks,
> Felipe

4 REINVENTION

VOCABULARY
Appearance

1 a Read the clues. Complete the crossword with words that describe appearance.

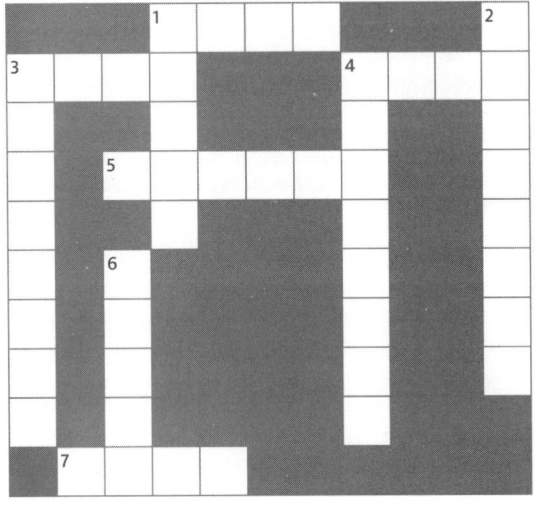

Across
1 This means 'without hair on your head'.
3 You have this kind of complexion if your skin is white or if you are not feeling well.
4 This describes light-coloured hair, e.g. blonde.
5 A hairstyle where your hair is cut in a horizontal line across your forehead.
7 When you change your hair colour using chemicals, you have hair like this.

Down
1 Men can grow this hair on their chin.
2 Lines you get on your skin as you get older.
3 If you wear jewellery in your ears or nose, you probably have one of these.
4 These are small brown marks that some people get on their skin.
6 Your hair is like this if it is not straight.

b Circle the word that <u>doesn't</u> work in each sentence.
1 I have *beards / freckles / wrinkles* around my nose.
2 My hair is naturally very *dyed / fair / dark*.
3 My sister doesn't have straight hair – it's *curly / pale / wavy*.
4 Would you ever get a *tattoo / piercing / complexion*?
5 Lots of men have a *bald / beard / moustache*.

2 Choose the correct options to complete the sentences.
1 My uncle's *growing / making* a moustache and it's already quite long.
2 We're going to the bathroom to *get / put* on our make-up.
3 My hair's getting quite long so I need to *do / get* a haircut.
4 Dirk looks great bald – that's why he always *cuts / shaves* his head.
5 I was going to *get / make* a piercing in my nose, but then I changed my mind.
6 If you want to *change / grow* your look, let's go shopping and get completely new clothes.

Describing people

3 Write the letters in brackets in the correct order to complete the words.

Hi Sharon
Sorry I haven't written for a while, but I've been really busy! Moving to the ballet school in Russia has been a complete life change. The teachers here are really strict. They're not at all as (1)_____ _____ (*dlia cabk*) as the ones back home in Brasilia! It's also difficult because my Russian is really bad and I never say anything. That's unusual for me because I'm really (2)_____ (*tyatch*) and (3)_____ (*ogutingo*), as you know! The worst thing is that because I was worried about the language, I was quite (4)_____-_____ (*flse oscioncus*) about my dancing at first, too.
Luckily, I'm sharing a room with Vladimir and he's great. He speaks perfect English and he's really (5)_____ (*iyttw*). He's introduced me to all his friends, who are all very (6)_____ (*villey*) and invite me to lots of parties! But don't worry – I haven't forgotten my studies. Vlad is really (7)_____ (*addecited*) like me so we spend a lot of time practising. In fact, because of his help, I've become a lot more (8)_____ (*ofncitend*), which is good because we have a big show next week!
Speak soon!
Roberto
P.S. Picture attached!

VOCABULARY EXTENSION
Work

4 a Read the text. Match the words in bold to definitions a–f.

Changing direction

This time last year, I was working at a big bank. Everything seemed perfect – I had just had a **promotion** and a pay rise. Then, my employers had to make a lot of people **redundant** – I lost my job and my high **salary**, and I didn't know what to do.

After a month of unsuccessful job applications, I started to work as a **freelance** writer. I asked my old boss for a **reference**, and he wrote a lot of positive things about me. Now I write blogs and articles about financial issues, and I've decided to **train** as a journalist. Losing my job forced me to change my career and I actually feel a lot happier now.

a having lost your job, because your employer no longer needed you. _____
b when you are given a better, more important job. _____
c to learn the skills needed for a particular job. _____
d a regular, fixed payment given to an employee. _____
e a statement describing a person's skills and work experience, written by a colleague. _____
f earning money by working for several different companies. _____

b Complete the chart with the words in bold in **5a**.

Nouns	Adjectives	Verbs

BRING IT TOGETHER

5 Complete the conversation with the words from the box. There is one word that you don't need.

chatty   dark   dedicated   dyed
laid back   lively   look   promotion
redundant   salary   shave

A Hi, Tina!

B Hi Tom! Wow, I love your profile photo! You've completely changed your (1)_____ since we were at school. Your clothes, hair, everything!

A It's true.

B Isn't your hair naturally (2)_____?

A Yeah, it's (3)_____ blonde now. Do you like it? I was going to (4)_____ my head this week, but I decided to change my hairstyle like this instead.

B Well, it suits you. So you're living the surfer lifestyle now?

A Yeah. It's a very nice, (5)_____ life, very relaxing.

B You're so lucky! I'm working in a bank and it's really stressful. I've just had a (6)_____ so my job is more important now, but I'm busy all the time. And no one talks at work. I hate that because I'm really (7)_____.

A But it's a good job, isn't it? I'm just giving surfing lessons. My (8)_____ isn't great, so I have to live with my parents.

B Are you studying as well?

A Yeah, I am. I'm studying drama. I've been really (9)_____ this year year. I've been working very hard! The lessons are really (10)_____ and energetic so it's fun.

B I studied Business Management – and that wasn't fun at all!

4

GRAMMAR
Present perfect or past simple?

1 Choose the correct options to complete the text.

(1)*You probably heard / You've probably heard* stories about how future stars were discovered in the street, but Alexander Beck's story is especially amazing. Earlier this year, the teenager (2)*ran into / has run into* fashion scout Cesar Perin in a Cambridge bookshop. Perin (3)*immediately noticed / has immediately noticed* Alexander's unusual look. From that moment, Alexander (4)*worked / has worked* with Perin as the latest top male model. He (5)*already appeared / has already appeared* in *Vogue* magazine, and has more big projects to come. His life (6)*changed / has changed* completely from the time when he was a normal schoolboy. In fact, before his modelling career, Alexander (7)*worked / has worked* in his local fish and chip shop! Since leaving that job, his income (8)*rose / has risen* enormously, as he now walks down the catwalk for Prada in fashion shows across Europe. In a time when it (9)*became / has become* almost impossible to turn on the TV without seeing competitions for 'the next top model', Alex's story is incredibly surprising. He (10)*didn't fight / hasn't fought* to appear on TV like thousands of other hopefuls – in fact, he had never considered modelling before that trip to the bookshop a few months ago.

2 Complete the sentences with *already* or *yet*.

1 Cora's on a diet. She's _____ lost a lot of weight.
2 Dean wants to get another tattoo. I think he's mad – he's got eight _____ !
3 Has Jim started his new job _____ ?
4 Julia's only 21, but she's _____ started using anti-ageing cream.
5 I really need a haircut, but I haven't been to the hairdresser's _____ .
6 Xana hasn't opened her new salon _____ , but I think it's going to be a great success!

3 a Complete the pairs of sentences using the words in brackets. In each pair, use one verb in the past simple and one verb in the present perfect.

1 i The new sunbed salon on King Street _____ (open) last week.   _b_
  ii The new sunbed salon on King Street _____ (not/open/yet). ___
2 i Olle _____ (shave) his head yesterday because he wanted to change his look. ___
  ii Olle _____ (never/shave) his head before, but now he wants a new look. ___
3 i I've started going to the gym, but I _____ (not/build up) my muscles yet. ___
  ii I've started going to the gym. I _____ (go) three times at the weekend! ___
4 i Julio's only 29, but his hair _____ (already/start) to go grey. ___
  ii Julio's only 29, but his hair _____ (go) grey when he was very young. ___

b Match pictures a–h to the sentences in **3a**.

Present perfect simple or continuous?

4 Complete the sentences with the correct form of the words in brackets: present perfect or present perfect continuous.

1. Maria's obsessed with having a tan. She _____ (go) to the sunbed salon three times already this week.
2. Gabrielle _____ (write) her autobiography – it's almost finished.
3. I _____ (have) four piercings since I was 18. I really regret getting them.
4. He _____ (grow) a beard for two weeks – it's getting quite thick.
5. Since she came out of prison, she _____ (try) to rebuild her image.
6. He _____ (direct) 15 films and is now working on his sixteenth.
7. She _____ (look) for a job for two months. I hope she'll get an interview soon.
8. Janine _____ (dye) her hair red, blue and green, but now it's her natural colour again.

5 Which sentences are correct? Tick (✓) the correct box: a, b or both a and b.

1. a I've had a haircut today.
   b I've been having a haircut today.
   a ☐   b ☐   both a and b ☐
2. a Wow! George has really changed his look!
   b Wow! George has really been changing his look!
   a ☐   b ☐   both a and b ☐
3. a He's written about his experiences as a tattoo artist.
   b He's been writing about his experiences as a tattoo artist.
   a ☐   b ☐   both a and b ☐
4. a José looks different because he's shaved his head.
   b José looks different because he's been shaving his head.
   a ☐   b ☐   both a and b ☐
5. a I'm looking for a job so I've sent ten emails this week.
   b I'm looking for a job so I've been sending ten emails this week.
   a ☐   b ☐   both a and b ☐
6. a The new campaign has gained support over the last few weeks.
   b The new campaign has been gaining support over the last few weeks.
   a ☐   b ☐   both a and b ☐

Uses of the *-ing* form

6 Change one word in each sentence to the *-ing* form.

1. *No smoke in school.*   smoking
2. The band's new song is all about reinvent yourself.
3. Use a sunbed to get a tan is very popular in many countries.
4. I can't get used to see her with purple hair!
5. Agapi is much better at English than me – her speak is really good.
6. If you want to improve your Spanish, have you considered have a holiday in Mexico?
7. I always enjoy watch French films on TV, though I can't always understand everything.
8. I'm looking forward to go to America so I can practise my English.

BRING IT TOGETHER

7 Choose the correct options to complete the text.

Crisis in the Carteret Islands

As climate change continues, the people of the Carteret Islands ⁽¹⁾*had / have had* to accept that their lives are going to change completely. For centuries, the women of the islands ⁽²⁾*have owned / have been owning* the land, and so today one woman, local leader Ursula Rakova, is working with her people to help them with this change. Due to rising sea levels, her own island of Huene ⁽³⁾*has disappeared / has been disappearing* beneath the sea – she can see the damage increasing all the time.

There are approximately 3,000 islanders and ⁽⁴⁾*moving / having moved* them all is an enormous task. Day by day, people ⁽⁵⁾*have been going / went* to Bougainville on the mainland to start a new life. However, ⁽⁶⁾*leaving / leave* their homes is difficult and many people feel desperate.

Since the sea levels began to rise, Ms Rakova ⁽⁷⁾*has been fighting / fought* to build new houses and schools for her people. After ⁽⁸⁾*waited / waiting* a long time for government help, she finally decided to lead the relocation programme herself. She ⁽⁹⁾*formed / has formed* her own charity in 2006 to tell the world about her people's crisis. Her message is clear. Although climate change ⁽¹⁰⁾*didn't affect / hasn't affected* every country yet, it is already destroying lives in many of the poorest parts of the globe.

Skills development

FUNCTIONAL LANGUAGE
Complaining

1 Put the words in brackets in the correct order to complete the conversations.

1 At home

A Oh no! They're playing music again.
B I know. (1)_____ (it's nerves really my on getting).
A And (2)_____ (playing that they're always song)! Don't they have any other CDs?
B They were playing music at three o'clock this morning.
A (3)_____ (me mad driving it's). I'm going to go round and complain.

2 At work

C I'm having real problems with my new clients. My contact person, Amy, calls me all the time – at night, at the weekend…
D That is a bit unreasonable. I will say something to her about it.
C Also, (4)_____ (way really it the me annoys) she tells me to do things. It's like she's my manager – not you.
D It sounds difficult, but they're important clients.
C I know, but (5)_____ (you never they thank say) for anything. They're really rude!

3 In a band

E I'm so tired of the band.
F Is it because of Mike?
E Yeah, it is. He's a great singer, but (6)_____ (the can't I way he stand) keeps giving orders to everyone.
F I know. (7)_____ (exactly on people strong skills not he's). He thinks he's the boss.
E And I started the band! It's my group – not his!
F (8)_____ (most the that thing me annoys) is that he never asks us about the songs. He just chooses them and we play them!
E Well I think we should leave the band and start a new one on our own!

LISTENING Prediction

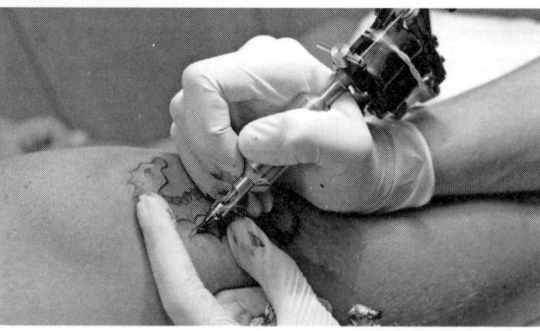

1 a You are going to listen to an interview with a tattoo artist from Macau. Look at the questions. What do you think the answers will be?

1 Why did you become a tattoo artist?
   _____
2 What kind of character do you need to be a tattoo artist?
   _____
3 What kind of people had tattoos in the past?
   _____
4 When do you refuse to tattoo someone?
   _____
5 What kind of images are popular as tattoos?
   _____
6 How do you feel about your job?
   _____

b 🔊 4.1 Listen and check your answers. How many of your predictions were correct?

2 a Complete the sentences.

1 My father and my grandfather were both tattoo artists, so it's kind of a _____ business.
2 Even today, if you go for a job _____ or something you might need to cover up your tattoo.
3 Just this _____ I spoke to a guy about his tattoo design and he changed his mind twice while he was talking to me.
4 A tattoo of a rabbit represents _____ , for example.
5 A tattoo of a _____ represents a fun or a lively person.
6 I enjoy helping people to change their _____ .
7 I see myself as part of a tradition going back _____ of years.

b Listen again and check your answers.

> **STRATEGY** Before listening to an audio, try to guess what the speaker will say. If you know the person's nationality, age, gender, profession, etc., it can help you to guess their opinions. Don't forget to look at any pictures for clues about the speaker.

Skills 4

Writing Informal writing

1 Read the email quickly and answer the questions.

1 What job has Jay got? _____
2 Who helped her to find the job? _____
3 How long did she have to wait for the result of her interview? _____

Hey everyone,

How's it going? You won't believe what I'm about to tell you. You know that I came home to Singapore last year after we were all studying in London? Well, I've been looking for work for ages, but I've finally found a job... I'm going to work for the police, as an interpreter!

It's kind of weird – doing police work is a big change from reading literature and writing essays! My dad saw the job advert in the paper and he told me to get in touch with them. At first I wasn't sure, but I did the interview... and they gave me the job there and then! It does help that I speak English, German, Chinese, Malay and 'Singlish' (our version of English – remember?). And using my languages is what I enjoy most, so I think the work will be interesting.

Anyway, the interview was crazy. I really dressed up – I took out all my piercings, washed the red dye out of my hair and put on this very uncool jacket. It was like my school uniform or something! My sister was so shocked by my 'transformation' that she took a photo of me (attached)!

Anyway, they must have liked it because I start the job on Monday. I reckon I'll only do it for a year or so, and then find something different. But a job's a job, right?!

Anyway, miss you!

Love,

Jay

2 Read the email again. Find informal equivalents for the formal words and phrases.

Formal	Informal
(1)Dear all	Hey everyone
(2)How are you?	
(3)a long time	
(4)slightly	
(5)to contact	
(6)immediately	
(7)unfashionable	
(8)I think	
(9)around 12 months	
(10)Best wishes	

3 Write a reply to Jay. Respond to her news and tell her about what you have been doing recently. Use ideas from the Strategy box to help you.

> **Strategy** When you write an informal email, you can
> - use informal words and expressions (*Hey, kind of, I reckon,* etc.)
> - use contractions (*I'm, I've, it's,* etc.)
> - use less formal punctuation like dashes (–) and exclamation marks (!)
> - use short or incomplete sentences and questions (*remember?, miss you!*).

5 FOOD FOR THOUGHT

VOCABULARY
Food

1 Put the letters in brackets in the correct order to make cooking words.

My Idea of Comfort Food – Margaret Foo

When I go home to Malaysia, there's one food that I always want: *nasi lemak*. It's our national dish, and my mother makes the best! It's rice which is (1)_____ (smeedat) with coconut milk and eaten with various ingredients like raw cucumber, spices and a (2)_____ (delibo) egg, as well as (3)_____ (tedroas) peanuts. It's really adaptable so many people eat it with other Malaysian dishes, like *rendang*. That's beef which is cooked for several hours to absorb special spices. I've even seen *nasi lemak* served in seaside towns as an accompaniment to seafood (4)_____ (legirdl) on a charcoal fire.

However, *nasi lemak* is most often eaten for breakfast – street vendors like the lady in the photo often sell it served in a banana leaf. If I can't get *nasi lemak*, I usually choose *roti canai*. It's a kind of bread, but it's not (5)_____ (kadeb) in an oven like Western bread. Instead it's (6)_____ (refid) in hot oil – it's delicious when served with condensed milk. Yum yum yum!

2 Circle the word that <u>doesn't</u> work in each sentence.
1 This chilli sauce is delicious, it's so *bland / spicy / sweet*.
2 This dessert isn't very good for your health because it's quite *creamy / crispy / greasy*.
3 I love this tropical lemon drink. It's quite *chewy / sweet / sour*, but really refreshing.
4 This soup doesn't taste very strong. In fact, it's quite *bland / mild / salty*.
5 When lettuce is fresh, it's perfect for a salad – really *bitter / crispy / crunchy*.

3 a Complete the words in the shopping lists for dishes 1–3.

1

tomatoes   spaghetti
(1) b _ _ _ l   (4) b _ _ _ _
(2) o _ _ _ _ o _ _   p _ _ _ _ r
(3) g _ _ _ _ c

2

apples   sugar
butter   (5) c _ _ n _ _ _ _ n
flour   (6) v _ _ _ _ _ a

3

chicken   (9) w _ _ _ _
(7) c _ _ _ _ _ i   v _ _ _ _ _ _ r
(8) s _ _ s _ _ _ _ green pepper
                (10) c _ r _ _ _ _ _ _ r

b Do you ever cook dishes like these?

Business

4 Match 1–6 to a–f.

1 Our customers always buy our jeans and no other company's
2 Most banks today have to be multinationals
3 You'll find chemists run by this company in every town in the country
4 My restaurant has another company's name
5 Our main target market is children aged 3–5
6 All the local book shops are closing

a because they can't compete with big internet shops.
b because it's one part of a franchise.
c because they're all part of a chain.
d because they love toys like this.
e because they have real brand loyalty.
f because they work in markets all over the world.

VOCABULARY EXTENSION
Cooking equipment

5 a Read the descriptions. Match items in the picture a–h to the words in bold in sentences 1–8.

1 A **wok** is used in Chinese cuisine to fry food at hot temperatures. ____
2 **Cutlery** is a group word for knives, forks and spoons. ____
3 A **saucepan** is used to boil food on top of the oven. ____
4 **Chopsticks** are two pieces of wood that people use for eating in many parts of the world. ____
5 Cut vegetables on a **chopping board** so the knife doesn't damage the rest of the kitchen. ____
6 To make vegetables into a soup, you turn them into liquid in a **blender**. ____
7 After you've cooked it, put the pasta in a **sieve** to get rid of the water. ____
8 Use a **frying pan** to make fried eggs or an omelette. ____

b 🔊 5.1 Listen and check.

BRING IT TOGETHER

6 Complete the blog post with words from the box. There is one word that you don't need.

> bitter bland blender brand loyalty
> compete creamy multinationals
> sieve target market vanilla vinegar

Soft Drinks Around the World

With globalisation, the big (1)____ like Coca-Cola and Pepsi seem to dominate the soft drinks industry. However, look a little further and you find many local drinks companies which are able to (2)____ with the big two. Here we profile some.

Asia is a key (3)____ for many drinks manufacturers. Korea's Milkis is popular both at home and abroad. It's made with milk, giving it a (4)____ taste. In Central America, Mexicans prefer Tonicol, a refreshing drink which is flavoured with (5)____.

If you don't like sweet drinks, Italy has a range of (6)____ ones, including Chinotto and Beverly (which tastes like tonic water). Finally, visitors to Brazil will be familiar with Guaraná. It's a fruity drink which enjoys huge (7)____ throughout the country – its sales there may be higher than those of Coca-Cola! So next time you're in a new place, why not try something different?

Alternatively, it's easy to make your own soft drinks – just liquidise some fruit in an electric (8)____. Put it through a (9)____ to remove the seeds, and in seconds, you'll have your own soft drink! Home-made drinks always taste great – they're full of flavour and never (10)____!

5

GRAMMAR
Future forms

1 Which sentences are correct? Tick (✓) the correct box: a, b or both a and b.

1. a I'm going to have dinner with my brother after work today.
   b I'm having dinner with my brother after work today.
   a ☐   b ☐   both a and b ☐

2. a There are fewer cacao farmers every year so I think the price of chocolate will continue to rise.
   b There are fewer cacao farmers every year so I think the price of chocolate is continuing to rise.
   a ☐   b ☐   both a and b ☐

3. a The sales meeting starts in five minutes.
   b The sales meeting's going to start in five minutes.
   a ☐   b ☐   both a and b ☐

4. a The new franchise will open next month – we need another meeting to finalise plans.
   b The new franchise is opening next month – we need another meeting to finalise plans.
   a ☐   b ☐   both a and b ☐

5. a That meal was delicious, Olle – I cook for you next week, I promise!
   b That meal was delicious, Olle – I'll cook for you next week, I promise!
   a ☐   b ☐   both a and b ☐

2 Replace the underlined verbs with either *will* or the present continuous for the future. (All of these sentences are already correct.) Write your answers below.

M Wow, Phueng, look at all these ingredients on your shopping list: chilli, garlic, coconut paste! What (1)<u>are you going to cook</u> with all of them? You've obviously got some interesting plans.

P (2)<u>I'm going to prepare</u> a green curry. It's a speciality of Thailand. (3)<u>Som and I are going to make</u> it for the end of course party.

M (4)<u>Isn't the chilli going to make</u> it a bit hot?

P Don't worry, Miranda. My curry (5)<u>isn't going to be</u> very spicy. (6)<u>It's going to taste</u> nice and mild.

M Great. Well, I think (7)<u>the other students are going to love it</u>.

P So that's my plan. What's yours?

M I don't have one. (8)<u>I'm not going to come</u> to the party.

P Really? Why not?

M (9)<u>I'm going to see</u> my sister tomorrow evening. She's just had her baby!

P Wow, that's great news!

M I'm sorry I won't be able to try the curry – I'm sure everyone will love it.

P Don't worry. I don't think (10)<u>we're going to eat</u> all of it, so I can save some for you to eat afterwards.

M Great! Thanks, Phueng!

1 _____   6 _____
2 _____   7 _____
3 _____   8 _____
4 _____   9 _____
5 _____   10 _____

Clauses

3 Choose the correct options to complete the sentences.

1. I'll go straight to the restaurant *as soon as / until* I've finished work.
2. You can't look at your mobile phone *before / once* the meeting begins.
3. We can't cook dinner *once / unless* we go to the supermarket!
4. Prices will continue to rise *after / until* food production costs go down.
5. Finish your main course *before / as soon as* you eat dessert, OK?
6. My journey to work takes two hours, so I usually have a coffee *after / until* I arrive.

4 Complete the sentences with the correct form of the words in brackets.

1. Don't buy food there unless you _____ it's fresh. (know)
2. As soon as the meeting _____ , call me. (finish)
3. Once Nadine _____ the USA, she can write her report about American food production. (visit)
4. I can't cook dinner until I _____ some meat and vegetables. (buy)
5. They won't open a franchise there unless the market _____ in the next few months. (change)
6. Dave will call you once he _____ a table in the restaurant. (have)
7. Let's have a coffee before we _____ . (leave)
8. Ask Iris to phone me after she _____ to the doctor. (speak)

Future continuous & future perfect

5 a Put the words in the correct order to make sentences.

1 be / people / tonight / will / making / 20 / Rita / for / dinner
   _____
2 started / 3 p.m. / Rita / cooking / will / by / have
   _____
3 have / arrived / seven / the / will / by / guests
   _____
4 by / eaten / everyone / will / a / eleven / lot / have
   _____
5 at / this / will / time / Rita / be / relaxing / tomorrow
   _____

b Which sentences in **5a** are
  a future continuous? _____   b future perfect? _____

6 Choose the correct options to complete the blog post.

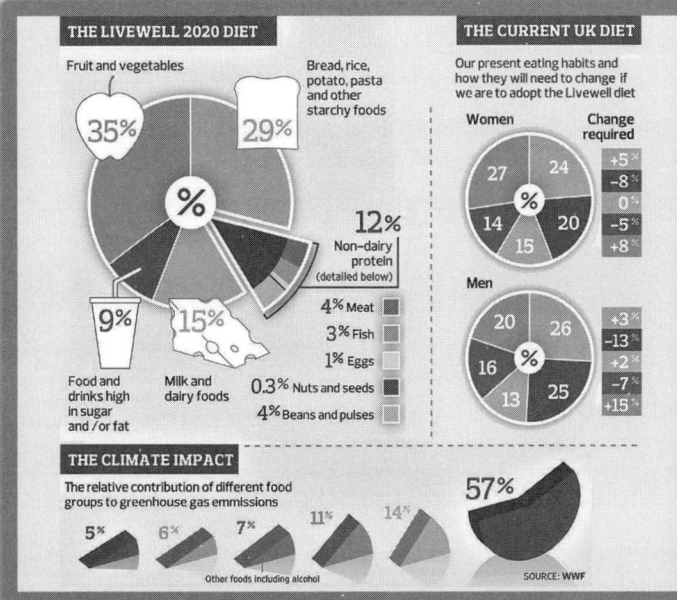

LIVE AND LET LIVE

By 2050, the world's population ⁽¹⁾*will be rising / will have risen* to 9 billion people. If that's true, by the middle of the century, large amounts of jungle ⁽²⁾*will already be turning into / will already have turned into* giant farms for meat and dairy production. After the disappearance of their forest homes, a large number of animal species ⁽³⁾*will be becoming / will have become* extinct, too.

How can we prevent that terrible future? One way is the WWF's Livewell diet. They hope more people ⁽⁴⁾*will be following / will have followed* it over the next few years. My family ⁽⁵⁾*will be trying / will have tried* this out for the next 12 months. On December 31, ⁽⁶⁾*we'll be finding out / we'll have found out* how easy it was to follow.

The idea is simple. If we reduce the amount of meat and dairy we eat, we can reduce the impact of farming on the environment. The WWF hopes the expansion of the world's farmland ⁽⁷⁾*will be stopping / will have stopped* completely by the end of 2050 – and our grandchildren ⁽⁸⁾*will still be enjoying / will still have enjoyed* the natural world.

BRING IT TOGETHER

7 a Read the magazine article. Choose the correct options 1–3 to complete Antonia's message.

Karim's Africa Questions

Dear Karim,
I ⁽¹⁾*'m travelling / will travel* to Mali next month. Before I ⁽²⁾*leave / 'm leaving*, I want to find out more about the local cuisine. ⁽³⁾*I'll be staying / I'll have stayed* in hotels and also with a local family.
Antonia

Antonia, your letter was delayed, so you'll already ⁽⁴⁾_____ arrived in Mali by the time my column appears – sorry! However, I hope that once you ⁽⁵⁾_____ read my reply, you'll know even more about Malian cuisine.
I expect that the family ⁽⁶⁾_____ cook a lot of meat dishes, like *yassa*. That's a spicy dish with onion and lemon. It's usually made with grilled chicken, ⁽⁷⁾_____ there is fish available. There's also *mafé*, beef boiled with peanuts. I have recipes for both, and ⁽⁸⁾_____ be uploading them to the website before the end of the week.
Couscous is also popular. When I go home to Mali, my mother cooks it for me almost as soon as I ⁽⁹⁾_____ walked through the door! It's real comfort food. Also look for *Meni-meniyang*, a sticky honey, butter and sesame dessert. Once ⁽¹⁰⁾_____ tried that, you won't want any other dessert. It's delicious!
Karim

b Complete Karim's reply with one word in each gap 4–10 (*don't*, etc. = one word).

Skills development

FUNCTIONAL LANGUAGE Checking understanding

1 a Complete the words to make a conversation.

A OK, we need to discuss what we have to do before we can open. George, have you looked into licensing?
B Sorry, (1)c_____ you s_____ that again?
A Licensing – we need to have a licence before we can open.
B Oh, I've applied and we should get a licence next month.
C So am I (2)r_____ in t_____ that we can't open before that?
A No, we can't. But there's still plenty to do! We need to decorate, buy furniture and source ingredients. George! Are you (3)f_____ ?
B Yes, sorry. (4)W_____ you say 'source ingredients', do you m_____ buy food?
A Yes, we want to find the best ingredients at the lowest prices. We need to meet suppliers and check out the local markets.
B Can I just (5)c_____ s_____? Are we still planning to only buy food within 30 kilometres of here?
A Yes, that's going to be our USP, isn't it?
B What (6)e_____ do you m_____ by USP?
A 'Unique selling point'. It's what makes us special. Does that make (7)s_____ ?
B Yes, completely. But what about drinks?
A Well, that's a bit more difficult. If we have the same policy for drinks, we'll only be able to serve water and apple juice! Do you (8)s_____ w_____ I mean?
B Hmm, yes, I agree. One (9)t_____ I don't u_____ , though, is who's going to do all the paperwork when we open – we'll all be so busy cooking and serving food.
A Good point, maybe we need to employ a manager ...

b What business are the people in **1a** planning to start? Tick (✓) the correct picture.

a

b

c

LISTENING Recognising context

1 a 🔊 5.2 Listen to five short conversations. Who is speaking? Number speakers a–e in the order that you hear them.

a colleagues ____
b a tour guide and some tourists ____
c a family ____
d a taxi driver and a customer ____
e a waiter and a customer ____

b Listen again. Answer the questions.

1 What kind of food does the restaurant serve in conversation 1?
_____
2 What are the people going to eat in conversation 2?
_____
3 What drink does the woman order in conversation 3?
_____
4 What is the boy going to eat first and second in conversation 4?
_____
5 How does Zahra describe the chicken dish in conversation 5?
_____

STRATEGY When you listen to people talking, try to understand the general situation. Who are the people? Where are they? How do they know each other? This can help you understand what they are saying.

Skills 5

Reading Guessing unknown words

1 Read 'The Story of Cinnamon'. Answer the questions.

1 Which island is mentioned in the text?

_____

2 Which two uses of cinnamon are mentioned?

_____

The Story of Cinnamon

In the Indian Ocean, there is an island so beautiful that its ancient name, Serendeep, gave us the modern word *serendipity* – to find something wonderful by chance. This island of lush tropical jungles and heavy rains also hid a great secret for thousands of years, for it was the only source of one of the world's most precious spices, cinnamon. Today the island is known as Sri Lanka.

Cinnamon is first mentioned in Chinese writing from 2700BC. Yet despite its long use, its origin was obscure. Ancient thinkers guessed that cinnamon was caught in fishing nets by sailors on the Nile. It was an Arab philosopher who first surmised that it was a product of the East. But what exactly is cinnamon? It's actually the bark of a tree. People take it off the outside of the tree and dry it on the ground where it curls up into tubes. Interestingly, today both plantation owners and workers share the profits of this trade. The workers get one-third of the sale price with the rest going to the landowner. Sharing the wealth encourages everyone to produce the best quality cinnamon.

Production of the spice is of enormous importance to Sri Lanka. Although it's no longer a luxury good, it is used in cooking worldwide. In the USA, people eat it with toasted bread, or use it to bake cakes. In the Middle East it is added to roast lamb, and it is boiled with meat and vegetables in traditional Persian stews.

However, the future does not look rosy. It is difficult to find workers to harvest the crop. People have been leaving the plantations to move to the city, a trend which will be increasing over future years. Older workers fear that within a generation people will have forgotten the skills needed to prepare cinnamon. This is worrying, as although the work is hard, producing cinnamon does pay well.

Perhaps all is not lost. Scientists are interested in the medicinal properties of cinnamon, and they will be experimenting with new ways of using it during next the few years. By the end of the decade, medicines based on cinnamon will have been developed to combat diabetes and it will also have been used to help produce chemicals for cancer research. So it seems there are still chapters to be written in the 5,000-year history of cinnamon.

2 a Read the text again. Look at the underlined words. What kind of words are they? Can you guess their meaning just from the information around them?

b Match the underlined words in **2a** to definitions 1–7.

1 a kind of heavy soup made with vegetables, meat, fish, etc. _____
2 the hard wooden 'skin' on the outside of a tree _____
3 the characteristics of a chemical or a substance _____
4 to guess something or make a conclusion based on facts and information _____
5 very green, with lots of plants _____
6 something that will probably be good _____
7 a farm (usually in a hot country) where bananas, sugar, etc. are grown _____

Strategy When you read a text, you probably won't understand every word. When you see a word you don't know, try to guess the meaning from context. What kind of word is it (noun, verb, etc.)? Look at the words before and after it. Do they help you understand the meaning? If you took the word out of the sentence, what word would you use in your language?

33

6 THAT'S ENTERTAINMENT

VOCABULARY
Entertainment

1 Complete the words.

So Giovanna, why did you become a clown?

For the money! No seriously, I used to work as a (1)b _ _ k _ r, playing guitar in the street. I also did a little act as a (2)m _ m _ a _ t _ _ _ _, you know, acting without words. One day a member of the (3)a _ d _ _ _ _ c _ told me that my act was really funny. He was a (4)m _ g _ _ _ i _ n doing tricks and illusions in the local circus – and he got me the job.

What's the best thing about being a clown?

Working with the other people. All the other circus (5)p _ _ f _ _ _ m _ _ s are really nice people. And the (6)m _ k _ -u _ artist who does my face makes me laugh so much before I go on stage. She could be a (7)s _ _ _ _ d-u _ comedian if she wanted.

What's the worst thing about being a clown?

People don't take you seriously.

Where do you see your career going?

My dream is to be a (8)s _ _ _ _ _ _ tw _ _ t _ r in the movies. I am working on a story now about some wooden (9)p _ pp _ _ ts who come to life and run away from the circus. My boyfriend is a (10)s _ _ n _ e _ g _ n _ _ _ _ for TV here in Montevideo and he knows the right people, so maybe I can get a director or someone to read it.

Well, we wish you the best of luck, Giovanna!

2 a Find ten film and theatre words in the word search.

L	S	S	C	R	I	P	T	S	A
H	O	V	F	Q	Z	H	J	P	W
I	U	Y	Z	J	B	C	F	E	P
P	N	K	X	M	H	A	X	C	E
A	D	H	R	W	W	S	X	I	R
R	T	P	L	O	T	T	F	A	F
T	R	M	Q	M	V	Z	Z	L	O
R	A	B	S	C	E	N	E	E	R
E	C	A	F	Y	K	O	J	F	M
C	K	Z	S	T	A	G	E	F	A
O	S	C	E	N	E	R	Y	E	N
P	O	U	S	D	T	L	A	C	C
G	I	Q	L	P	O	R	W	T	E
V	D	M	E	B	T	T	S	S	L

b Match the words from **2a** to the definitions. There are two words that you don't need.

1 Part of a film or TV show where all the action happens in one place, like a chapter in a book. s_____
2 All the actors who are working on a play or a film. c_____
3 The written words of a film or TV series that the actors must learn. s_____
4 A role played by one actor in a film or TV series. p_____
5 Amazing images or scenes in a film, made with computers or models, etc. s_____ e_____
6 The story of a film, book or play. p_____
7 All the music and songs in a film. s_____
8 The place where the actors stand when they are acting in the theatre. s_____

3 Circle the word that <u>doesn't</u> work in each sentence.

1 I found this film really *action-packed / memorable / moving*, even though its plot is very simple.
2 We felt great after watching this film. It was really *hilarious / depressing / uplifting*.
3 This crime movie is really *gripping / intriguing / predictable* – you'll never guess how it ends!
4 I didn't enjoy the film at all. I thought it was *unrealistic / hilarious / depressing*.
5 The start of the film is really *action-packed / unrealistic / memorable*. I was very impressed by the first scene.

34

Noun-building suffixes

4 Complete the sentences with the noun form of the word in brackets.

1. Making the film wasn't a lot of fun because there was a lot of _____ between the cast and the director. (tense)
2. She's a great actress, but she has one _____ : she's not very good at comedy. (weak)
3. The new science fiction movie is creating a lot of _____ at the moment. (excite)
4. Is there a cinema in this _____ ? (neighbour)
5. You need a lot of _____ to be a successful set designer in the theatre. (create)
6. I loved Japanese cartoons in my _____ . (child)
7. The plot is very hard to follow – it caused a lot of _____ in the audience! (confuse)

Computer games

5 Choose the correct options to complete the text.

Nowadays every (1)*first / one* person game seems to be based on killing, so you'd think the most popular computer games character would be some soldier from a violent (2)*gun / shoot* 'em up. In fact, it's a friendly Italian plumber called Mario, Nintendo's megastar.

Mario first appeared in a classic (3)*platform / station* game for arcades: *Donkey Kong*. In the game, players (4)*go / make* up a level after dodging barrels thrown at them by a giant ape. It was completely addictive as people progressed from one (5)*ladder / stage* to the next. Its simple (6)*drawings / graphics* explain Mario's distinctive red and blue costume: those bright colours made him easier to see.

Mario is popular with children as well as adults so he's often the star in each new Nintendo (7)*apparatus / console*, like the Wii. One of their biggest sellers was 2008's *Super Mario Kart*, where players race on a (8)*divided / split* screen. The game's innovation was its steering wheel: players slot their handheld (9)*controller / remote* into the back of it. Then the machine can (10)*'look' / 'read'* their movements using sophisticated motion (11)*alarms / sensors*, just like they're driving a car. Nintendo fans agree that the Mario games have always provided excellent (12)*gameplay / game pleasure*, from the birth of the Mario character in 1981, right up to the present day!

■ VOCABULARY EXTENSION
Further noun forms

6 a Complete the chart with ten film and theatre jobs. Add the suffixes in the table to the root words in the box.

~~act~~   cartoon   comedy   compose   criticise
direct   drama   illustrate   music   produce

-ian	-er/-or	-ist	-ic
	actor		

b 6.1 Listen and check.

7 Complete the sentences with the correct form of nouns from **6a**.

1. The play was very popular with the public, but the _____ didn't like it.
2. George is so funny – he really should be a(n) _____ .
3. Writing music is tough – not many _____ make a living from it.
4. Someone who writes plays is known as a(n) _____ .
5. You have to be good at drawing to be a(n) _____ or a(n) _____ .
6. Some people think that the _____ and the _____ of a film are more important than the cast.

BRING IT TOGETHER

8 Complete the email with the words from the box. There is one word that you don't need.

actor   audience   circus   console   controllers   critic
hilarious   magician   neighbourhood   part   script

Hi Yvain!

How are you doing? I'm writing to tell you about Fadiya's play. It was an amazing success. There were about 200 people in the (1)_____ – I think almost everyone in the (2)_____ had decided to come and see it. There was even a theatre (3)_____ from the regional paper! Fadiya wrote the (4)_____ and she directed the play, too. It's about a group of (5)_____ performers and their lives as they travel around the country. The (6)_____ is getting older and he's losing his ability to do tricks and illusions. At the same time, a young puppeteer is becoming really successful because his part of the show is (7)_____ – people find his act really funny and the magician is jealous. I played one of the clowns from the circus. It was a small (8)_____ , but a lot of fun.

There was only one problem on the night when I was supposed to be playing on a games (9)_____ with another character. They had forgotten to put the (10)_____ on the stage, so we had nothing in our hands! We just carried on and I don't think anyone noticed – I hope not, anyway!

If you want to see some photos, they're up on our website. I bet my clown costume will make you laugh!

Speak soon, Natalia

6

GRAMMAR
The passive voice

1 Put the words in the correct order to make sentences.

1 in / play / the / set / is / Thailand

2 be / month / the / released / will / next / film

3 Hitchcock / by / directed / was / film / the

4 the / was / Cruz / role / for / starring / Penelope / chosen

5 being / by / Clooney / written / George / script / the / is

6 been / the / given / TV / has / programme / reviews / great

2 a Rewrite these sentences, as in the example. The first word is given.

1 They chose Clint Eastwood for the lead role in *A Fistful of Dollars*.
   Clint Eastwood <u>was chosen for the lead role in A Fistful of Dollars.</u>

2 They use Glasgow as the setting for a lot of films nowadays.
   Glasgow _____ .

3 Many people think that *Citizen Kane* is the best film of all time.
   It _____ .

4 People say that you can see a modern plane in the 1963 film *Cleopatra*.
   It _____ .

5 The Japanese company Studio Ghibli made the film *Spirited Away*.
   Spirited Away _____ .

6 In the 1920s, people thought that colour films were impossible to make.
   In the 1920s, it _____ .

7 Many countries banned the film *A Clockwork Orange*.
   The film _____ .

8 They believe that saying the name of the play *Macbeth* is unlucky in theatre.
   It _____ .

b Which sentences in **2a** refer to
i facts? _____
ii opinions? _____

3 Correct the sentences. Tick (✓) two correct sentences.
1 We were told that the film was sold out.
2 The play has been received a lot of praise.
3 I have invited to the premiere of the latest Tom Cruise film.
4 The song was written of Paul McCartney.
5 The part of Sherlock Holmes is be played by Benedict Cumberbatch.
6 The performance is going to be cancel because of the bad weather.
7 It is think that people will stop buying DVDs in the future.
8 A scene from the movie is being shot in the City Museum today.

4 Complete the text with the correct passive form of the verbs in brackets.

Spotlight on… Hong Kong Movies

For many years now, the Hong Kong film industry (1)_____ (know) for its martial arts films and exciting action movies. It (2)_____ (also / admire) for a long time for its output: in 2009, over 50 films (3)_____ (produce). However, the Hong Kong film industry is now getting a new kind of recognition. In 2008, American movie *The Departed* won the Best Picture Oscar. The film (4)_____ (base) on a 2002 Hong Kong hit, *Infernal Affairs*. The remake was a double success for director Martin Scorsese, who finally picked up the Best Director Oscar after he (5)_____ (beat) to the award several times before. Suddenly, everyone was talking about Hong Kong film.

It (6)_____ (think) that the local film industry will continue to grow in future. Foreign interest in Hong Kong movies (7)_____ (encourage) by the recent international success of superstars like Chow Yun-Fat, who appears in 2012's *The Monkey King*. Nowadays, local film makers (8)_____ (give) more and more government funding: with its combination of talent, energy and government support, it's clear that Hong Kong will be one of the places to watch over the next few years. You heard it here first!

Have something done

5 Match a–b to i–ii.

1. a The circus performers had their tent put up ___
   b The circus performers put their tent up ___
   i by themselves because it was a small circus company.
   ii by a team who worked for them.
2. a The composer recorded his new song ___
   b The composer got his song recorded ___
   i by a professional sound engineer.
   ii using his own equipment.
3. a The director had the script rewritten ___
   b The director rewrote the script ___
   i by a new scriptwriter.
   ii without anybody's help.
4. a We're a small theatre so the actors put ___
   b On a movie set, the actors have their make-up put ___
   i on by a make-up artist.
   ii on their own make-up.
5. a Simon translated his play into Chinese ___
   b Simon had his play translated into Chinese ___
   i by a writer from Guangzhou.
   ii by using a dictionary and the internet.
6. a He got the scenery built ___
   b He built the scenery ___
   i by a team of backstage workers.
   ii himself to save money.

6 a Write sentences using the correct form of the verb in brackets.

1. I / have / my red carpet dresses / by top designers (make)
2. I / get / special shoes / to me / from Paris (send)
3. I / always / have / my face / white / before / I go / on stage (paint)
4. I / have / silk scarves, flowers and a rabbit / to me / before my act (bring)
5. I / have / had / my reviews / in national newspapers (publish)

b Who do you think said the sentences in 6a? Match them to the people.

a a magician ___
b a film star ___
c a theatre critic ___
d a mime artist ___
e a ballerina ___

BRING IT TOGETHER

7 Complete the text with one word in each gap (*don't*, etc. = one word).

Kite crazy in Afghanistan

Today, the skies above Kabul (1)___ filled with hundreds of colourful papers. It's autumn and Afghanistan's kite-flying season has just begun. For many years, kite flying had (2)___ banned and it has only recently (3)___ permitted again, which is great news for its followers. Even during the ban, kites (4)___ being produced secretly in hidden workshops, but now real shops (5)___ being opened again all over the city. That's not surprising because kite flying is an Afghan obsession. A kite is flown (6)___ two people: one controlling the string and the other the movement of the kite. They (7)___ used in contests like 'kite fighting' where players try to cut the string of the other person's kite. If they succeed, and the string gets (8)___ , the kite flies away into the air. These kites can (9)___ claimed by anyone in the city. That's OK because most of them are very cheap, although some serious players (10)___ their kite specially made by experts. Whoever makes them, the kites almost always have bright, dynamic designs – and some people hang them on the walls as decorations!

Skills development

FUNCTIONAL LANGUAGE Generalising

1 Complete the words in the conversations.

1 A What kind of people take the film-making course?
  B Well, a _ a r _ _ e, people already have some experience in the film industry, but it's not essential.

2 A How does your group find gigs?
  B What o _ _ _ n h _ _ p _ _ _ s is that we go to concerts and then we ask the people there if they are interested in hearing our band.

3 A How often do you use the games console?
  B We only use it when we have parties, g _ _ _ r _ _ _ _ y s _ _ _ k _ _ _ g. We don't play the games on our own much.

4 A Why do people take up salsa dancing as a hobby?
  B M _ r _ o _ t _ _ _ t _ _ _ n n _ _ _ people just do it because it's fun and a good way to keep fit.

5 A How do you meet people who do the same hobby as you – making animated films?
  B I _ 's o _ t _ _ _ the c _ s _ that I've run into them at conferences and fairs. There are always loads of other animators there.

6 A Do people often get hurt performing these circus tricks?
  B Oh no. I _ m _ s _ c _ s _ s, people are really careful. Accidents are very rare.

LISTENING Intonation

1 🔊 6.2 Listen to two conversations. Tick (✓) 1, 2 or both.

In which conversation	1	2	both
a do the speakers know each other well?			
b has someone lost something?			
c do they talk about a film?			
d do they talk about a game?			
e do they talk about making things?			

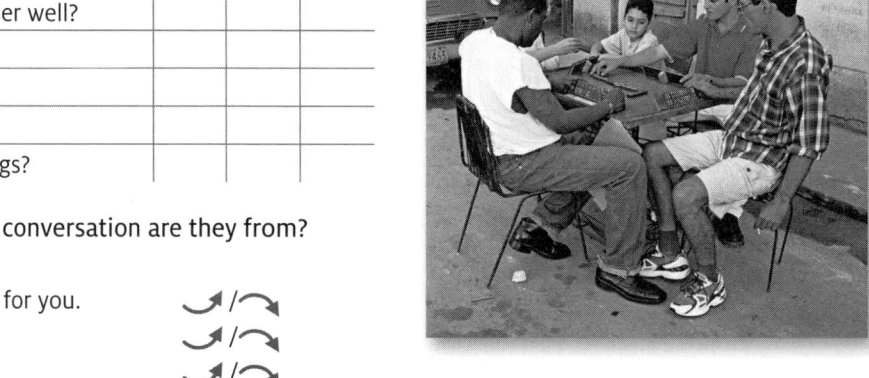

2 a Look at sentences 1–6. Which conversation are they from? Write 1 or 2.

a ☐ That must be really hard for you. ↗/↘
b ☐ It's a great film. ↗/↘
c ☐ They're beautiful! ↗/↘
d ☐ I'd love to have a go! ↗/↘
e ☐ I'm really sorry, but I can't. ↗/↘
f ☐ It would be awful if you didn't have it. ↗/↘

b Read the information in the Strategy box. Do you think the speaker will use rising (↗) or falling (↘) intonation in the sentences? Circle the correct answers.

3 a Listen again and check your answers in **2**.

b In which conversation is one of the speakers not saying exactly what he/she means? How do you know?

> **STRATEGY** When you listen, think about how a speaker says something (their intonation), as well as what he/she says.
> • When people feel happy or enthusiastic about something, they usually use rising (↗) intonation.
> • When they express sympathy about something, they usually use falling (↘) intonation.
> • Remember that sometimes people don't say exactly what they mean, perhaps because they are trying to be polite, or to make a joke. In this case, instead of rising or falling, their intonation often remains flat.

SKILLS 6

WRITING Summarising a plot

The Year of the Hare (Jäniksen vuosi)
by Arto Paasilinna

The Year of the Hare is a novel by Finnish author Arto Paasilinna. It's set in modern-day Finland, in both the capital Helsinki and the country's deep, northern forests. It's a heart-warming tale about Vatanen, a journalist, whose whole life changes after an encounter with a wild hare.

When the story opens, Vatanen is travelling with a photographer colleague. One night, they hit a hare with their car. The injured animal escapes into the forest, and when Vatanen goes to look for it, the photographer drives off, leaving him alone.

While Vatanen is looking after the frightened and injured hare, he makes an important decision. He decides to leave his hectic life in the city and travel the country with the animal as his companion. Following the news that he will not be returning to work, his wife and colleagues come to look for him. However, Vatanen refuses to return to his previous life. Instead, he begins an extraordinary road trip towards the Arctic Circle, always travelling with the hare by his side. His adventures include encounters with wild bears and forest fires, as well as an accidental trip into Russian territory.

The main character, Vatanen, is middle-aged and depressed. He is tired of writing unmemorable lifestyle articles for magazines and wants to taste real freedom. As he meets the people who live in the forests, like park rangers and farmers, he discovers that life has meaning all over again.

Combining a road trip with a story of personal discovery, *The Year of the Hare* is a pleasant story about how people can change direction, and return to a simpler, more natural way of life.

---

1 Read the plot summary quickly. Tick (✓) the information that it contains.
- ☐ the beginning of the story
- ☐ the end of the story
- ☐ where the story happens
- ☐ the names of all the characters
- ☐ the main events of the story
- ☐ the writer's opinion of the story
- ☐ a physical description of the main character
- ☐ the main theme/idea of the book

2 Complete the phrases. Then check your answers in the text.
1. It's s_____ in modern-day Finland
2. It's a heart-warming t_____ about
3. When the story o_____
4. W_____ Vatanen is looking after the frightened and injured hare
5. F_____ the news that he will not be returning to work
6. His a_____ include encounters with wild bears and forest fires
7. C_____ a road trip with a story of personal discovery

3 Write a plot summary of a book or a film that you know well. Use the paragraph plan to help you.

Paragraph 1: Where/When is it set? Who is the main character?

Paragraph 2: How does the story begin? What is the most important event in the book?

Paragraph 3: describe one or two further events

Paragraph 4: describe the main character's personality

Paragraph 5: conclusion – explain the main theme

STRATEGY When you write a plot summary of a book or film:
- use the present simple to summarise the main events of the story
- don't include all the events of the story. Focus on one or two key scenes
- use sequencing expressions (e.g. *first*, *while*, *following*) to show the order of events
- only describe one or two main characters. Concentrate on their personality, and don't include physical description
- in your conclusion, summarise the main themes or 'big ideas' of the story.

PROGRESS TEST 2

GRAMMAR & VOCABULARY
(25 points)

1 Complete the sentences with the correct form of the word in brackets. *(10 points)*

0 I have <u>known</u> (know) Ximena for over five years now.
1 Don't send that email! I _____ (finish) writing it yet!
2 It's time you came out of the water and had something to eat. You _____ (swim) for hours now!
3 Everyone's looking forward to _____ (see) you when you visit next month.
4 Waris can't take the exam unless he _____ (register) online.
5 Read the sign – No _____ (eat) in the computer room.
6 We're in a taxi, but the traffic's not moving. We _____ (miss) our flight!
7 By the end of the month, you _____ (work) here for 15 years.
8 I had my wallet _____ (steal) at the train station.
9 It _____ (believe) that there are many undiscovered animal species in the sea.
10 Once Clarissa _____ (read) your report, she'll want to ask you about it.

2 Circle the option that <u>doesn't</u> work. *(7 points)*

0 I love your (bald) / *dark* / *wavy* hair!
1 Zack looks completely different now that he's grown a *beard* / *complexion* / *moustache*.
2 Do you think Sofia has put on *freckles* / *make-up* / *weight*?
3 The pictures in the book were drawn by a(n) *cartoonist* / *illustrator* / *producer*.
4 I like to use herbs like *coriander* / *cinnamon* / *basil* in my cooking.
5 Apples taste best when they're *crunchy* / *sweet* / *creamy* and juicy.
6 The film was terrible. It was really *intriguing* / *predictable* / *unrealistic*.
7 I felt sad at the end of the play because it was so *depressing* / *gripping* / *moving*.

3 Read the definitions. Write the correct words. *(8 points)*

0 This describes a film that makes you feel very happy and positive at the end. u<u>plifting</u>
1 These are lines on your face that you get as you become older. w_____
2 This verb means to cook in hot water. b_____
3 This word can be used to describe the taste of coffee or lemon. b_____
4 You eat with these two pieces of wood in many parts of the world. c_____
5 This is a company which does business in many different countries. m_____
6 This is a musician or other entertainer who performs in the street. b_____
7 This is the story of what happens in a book, film, play, opera, etc. p_____
8 This is the time in your life between being a baby and a teenager. c_____

READING *(25 points)*

1 Read the text on page 41 and find five jobs that Tom Shadyac has done in the entertainment business. *(5 points)*

_____ _____ _____
_____ _____

2 Correct six mistakes in this summary of the article. *(6 points)*

After directing a series of unsuccessful movies, Tom Shadyac decided to change his life. He sold his apartment in Hollywood and moved into a trailer, and started to hand his money out to people in the street. Nowadays, he thinks no one's work is important in the movies, and so he has completely changed his outlook on life. He astonished the host of The Oprah Winfrey Show with his story, but he says he has no regrets, and is now a student at a university in Southern California.

3 Answer the questions, according to the article. *(14 points)*

1 Which movie stars has Tom Shadyac worked with?
   _____
2 What kinds of film has Shadyac made?
   _____
3 What event made him change his life?
   _____
4 What kind of people appear in *I am*?
   _____
5 What TV programmes did he appear on?
   _____
6 What skill does he now teach other people?
   _____
7 How does Shadyac feel since he gave away his fortune?
   _____

TEST 2

I am Tom Shadyac...

Imagine you were a Hollywood film director, responsible for hit movies like *Patch Adams* (with Robin Williams in the title role) or *The Nutty Professor* (starring Eddie Murphy). What would you do next? Probably not what Tom Shadyac did. He sold his Hollywood mansion and most of his possessions and moved into a trailer (a simple kind of mobile home). He gave it all up to live a simple life, and then made a film of his experiences, *I am* (2011).

This documentary tells how Shadyac chose a new direction in life after he was badly hurt in a bicycle accident. It convinced him to give up the pressure of his Hollywood life.

I am shows his interviews with various gurus and philosophers, such as Noam Chomsky, as he tries to find the meaning of life. For Shadyac, this means showing respect to everyone. He says now that as the director of a film, his role is no more important than anyone else from the sound engineer to the cleaner. Everyone's work is important.

This is very different to the usual way of thinking in the movie business, but Shadyac has more surprises, too. Earlier this year, he astonished the audience on *The Oprah Winfrey Show* by telling them that he had given away most of his fortune to charity.

Shadyac is one of those people who is successful at everything he does. Once he got his degree from UCLA Film School, he was quickly identified as a future talent. He began his career as an actor, working on small-screen shows like *Magnum PI*. Later, he moved into directing, and also became a producer on his latest films.

As a filmmaker his speciality is humour, something he developed as a stand-up comedian early in his career. This has also been useful when he has taken on the role of scriptwriter on his projects such as *Ace Ventura*, starring world-famous Jim Carrey. That's one part of his life that he hasn't given up, as he now instructs people how to write top-quality scripts at Pepperdine University in Southern California.

Despite giving up all that money, Shaydac insists he is happier now than he ever was when he was at the top of the Hollywood tree.

LISTENING (25 points)

1 🔊 T2 Listen to a podcast about a computer game, *Cooking Mama World Kitchen*. Tick (✓) the things that are mentioned. *(9 points)*

- [ ] console
- [ ] controller
- [ ] first person
- [ ] the gameplay
- [ ] characters
- [ ] graphics
- [ ] platform
- [ ] motion sensor
- [ ] shoot 'em up

2 Listen again. Are the sentences true (T) or false (F)? Correct the false sentences. *(16 points)*

1 *Cooking Mama World Kitchen* was invented in 2011 for the Nintendo DS. T / F

2 You can cut ingredients with a knife as part of the game. T / F

3 On the podcast, they talk about frying and grilling ingredients. T / F

4 *Cooking Mama* now offers 3D gameplay. T / F

5 Jake thinks that the character of Mama is too serious. T / F

6 Jake made some biscuits using a recipe from *Cooking Mama*. T / F

7 Leila's hamburger was eaten by Mama. T / F

8 Leila thinks *Cooking Mama* is a good game to play on your own. T / F

WRITING (25 points)

1 Complete the words in the email. *(5 points)*

Hi Alessandra

⁽⁰⁾ _H o w_ are you? ⁽¹⁾G _ _ s _ who I met the other day? Tanja – from our old jewellery-making course, remember? I hadn't seen her ⁽²⁾s _ _ _ _ the end of the course. I can't ⁽³⁾b _ _ i _ _ _ _ how much she's changed!
She's ⁽⁴⁾s _ _ _ _ I really thin, but she now has dyed blonde hair. And she wears this amazing handmade jewellery too – she has a really individual ⁽⁵⁾ _ _ _ k. I took a photo of us on my phone (I've attached it to this email). Check out her web page online – she's now working as a make-up artist in the film industry!
Bye for now,
Kim

2 You meet an old classmate that you haven't seen for a long time. Your classmate has completely changed his/her appearance, and job. Write an email to a friend telling them about him/her. *(20 points)*

7 SOCIETY AND YOU

VOCABULARY
Rules & behaviour

1 Complete the words in the conversation.

A What does that sign say?

B It says that it's (1)i __ l __ g __ l to release animals into the river.

A Why would someone do that?

B Lots of people get the wrong pet. They buy a baby turtle, for example, and they don't realise that it's a completely (2)__ __ ap __ op __ __ __ te pet for a city apartment. It soon grows very large, and they don't have the space for it, so they put it in a river. It's really (3)i __ r __ __ p __ ns __ b __ e.

A But putting it into the river doesn't do any harm, does it?

B Yes, it does! The animal could destroy the entire habitat. Dumping pets in the river is completely (4)u __ a __ c __ __ t __ b __ __ . People should find other homes for them instead. It's really (5)u __ r __ as __ n __ b __ e to think that a pet will be able to survive in the wild.

A That's true. I know my aunt's cat wouldn't survive a minute without her!

2 Complete the sentences with the correct form of the word in brackets.

1 You shouldn't use your credit card on that website. It doesn't look very _____ . (trust)

2 This GPS is _____ ! It can't find any of the addresses I need! (use)

3 If you can be _____ , you can often get cheaper flights by changing the day you leave or arrive. (flex)

4 Jimmy was being really _____ when he said he wouldn't obey the dress code. (child)

5 Do you know a _____ builder? We need someone to redo our kitchen. (rely)

6 I'm always very _____ when I wash these glasses as I don't want to break them. (care)

Bureaucracy

3 Complete the sentences with the correct phrases from the box.

| birth certificate   course enrolment form |
| formal complaint form   job application |
| passport application   proof of address |
| tax return |

1 Your _____ shows when and where you were born and who your parents are.

2 If you want to open a bank account, you have to provide _____ to show where you live.

3 I was very unhappy with the service I got so I asked for a _____ .

4 It can take a long time to fill in a _____ because there are usually a lot of questions about your work experience.

5 To find out how much money you owe the government, you need to fill in a _____ .

6 When I started at the college, I had to fill in a _____ .

7 I need to complete this _____ because I have to go abroad later this year.

Collective nouns

4 Which words from the box can you use to describe 1–7?

| crew   flock   gang   herd |
| horde   mob   pack   swarm |

1 A large group of pigeons _____

2 A large group of people protesting violently in the street _____ , _____

3 A group of children or teenagers who spend time together _____

4 An enormous number of mosquitoes flying together _____

5 A group of wolves or wild dogs _____

6 The people who work together on a plane _____

7 A group of buffalo _____

VOCABULARY EXTENSION
Further prefixes

5 a Read the definitions. Then complete the words in 1–5. Use the same prefix for both a and b.

inter-	between two things
mis-	wrongly, badly
over-	too much, more than usual
re-	again, repeated
under-	not enough, less than usual

1 a Our team was _____ confident. We thought it would be easy to win the football game, so we didn't play hard enough – and we lost!
  b Your holiday plans are completely _____ ambitious. You can't travel all round Mexico in a week!
2 a The suffix -ful is frequently _____ spelt as 'f-u-l-l'.
  b He was often _____ understood because he didn't communicate very clearly and he was very shy.
3 a The shop wouldn't sell my cousin the DVD because it was for over-18s and she was _____ age.
  b The vegetables are a bit _____ done. Let's put them back in the oven for 20 minutes.
4 a Synonyms are words that are _____ changeable. They mean the same thing.
  b We're going on an _____ continental flight between the US and Brazil.
5 a These are the _____ designed business cards. Do you like them better than the original ones?
  b Those jam jars are _____ usable, so don't throw them away. I'll use them when I make my own jam.

b 🔊 7.1 Listen and check.

6 Complete the sentences with words from **5a**.
1 The _____ website is much easier to use than the old one, and it looks better, too.
2 My name was _____ on my boarding card, so they wouldn't let me on the plane.
3 It's important that we have _____ products for all our mobile phones. If a gadget works with one phone, it should work with all of them.
4 Kemal failed his driving test because he was _____ and didn't prepare enough for it.
5 This steak is really _____. It's red! I can't eat that!
6 Most plastic bags are _____, so I don't know why we throw so many away.
7 There are lots of _____ airlines operating between Amsterdam and destinations in Asia.
8 The government has these really _____ plans. They won't be able to do everything in just five years!
9 Frederick is writing a book, but nobody likes it. He doesn't care because he thinks he's a _____ artist and that people will recognise his talent in the future!
10 They wouldn't let us into the nightclub because they thought we were _____ – and we didn't have our ID cards!

BRING IT TOGETHER

7 Complete the posts with words from the box. There are two words that you don't need.

careful   disrespectful   flexible
flock   helpful   ID card   illegal
intercontinental   gang   overconfident
passport application   unacceptable

Niko: When I moved here I needed to get a(n) (1)_____ because it's (2)_____ to live here without one. I waited at the office for nearly three hours, which I thought was completely (3)_____. Finally I got the form, and someone told me how to fill it in and was really (4)_____. Has anyone else had an experience like this?

Brendan: Once when I was on holiday I was walking down a busy street when a (5)_____ of men suddenly surrounded me, and one of them stole my passport. It was awful because I wasn't expecting it. I think I was (6)_____ – I had heard stories about this kind of thing but I didn't think it would happen to me. I went to the Irish Embassy, and they were really nice and helped me fill in a(n) (7)_____, so I was able to carry on with my holiday.

Min: Last year, I moved from Vietnam to the States. It was a(n) (8)_____ flight and we could only take 25 kilos of luggage. I was really (9)_____ when I packed my bags but they were still 30 kilos. Luckily, the man at the check-in desk said he would be (10)_____ with the rules for me because I was going to live in the US. I thought that was really kind of him.

7

Grammar

Past modals: *should have/could have*

1 a Put the words in the correct order to make sentences.

1 your you should you passport have with
   _____

2 for a asked formal could have complaint you form
   _____

3 fined having they a for him car have could dirty
   _____

4 shorts worn have temple to shouldn't I visit the
   _____

5 if she photos Iris was to should have allowed take asked
   _____

6 we problem have could a
   _____

b Which sentences in **1a** are in

1 the present? _____
2 the past? _____

2 Complete the conversations with the correct form of the words in brackets.

1 A I didn't get the job.
   B Well, you _____ more time on your application. You did it too quickly. (should/spend)

2 A That man was driving much too fast! This is the city centre!
   B I know! He _____ someone. (could/hurt)

3 A I've just discovered my passport's expired!
   B Oh no! We _____ the expiry date before we booked our flights. (should/check)

4 A They wouldn't let me in the cathedral because I was wearing shorts.
   B Oh dear! I _____ you they don't allow you in if you're in shorts. I went there last year. (could/tell)

5 A I can't believe the airport staff charged me $40 for excess baggage!
   B Well, you _____ so much luggage. You'll never wear all those clothes in two weeks! (should/bring)

6 A Did you finish filling in your tax return in the end?
   B Yes, finally! Thank you so much – I _____ it without your help. (could/finish)

3 Correct the sentences. Tick (✓) one correct sentence.

1 You should have check the form before you sent it in.
2 We should changed our clothes before we went to visit the temple.
3 You shouldn't have downloaded that film.
4 You couldn't went to work yesterday – you were too ill.
5 We could park outside the station, but we parked in the car park instead.
6 Anton should have driven as much as possible next week to prepare for his driving test.

Past modals: speculation & deduction

4 a Look at the photo and responses 1–4. What do you think the man looking for?

1 Are you sure you packed it? You **might have left** it at home.

2 Oh no, it **must have fallen** out of your bag!

3 You **can't have lost** it. I saw you put it in your bag after we went through passport control.

4 Check your bag again. You **might not have looked** properly.

b Look at the words in bold in responses 1–4. Match them to uses a–d.

a a speculation about something we are sure happened _____
b a speculation about something we think happened _____
c a speculation about something we think didn't happen _____
d a speculation about something we are sure didn't happen _____

44

5 Rewrite the sentences using the words in bold. Keep the same meaning.

1 I'm sure they liked my job application because I've got an interview next week. **must**
   They must have liked my job application because I've got an interview next week.

2 I don't believe that Lucas went to Chile. **can't**
   _____

3 I think my job application got lost in the post because I haven't received a reply. **must**
   _____

4 Maybe Jack didn't know about the dress code. **have**
   _____

5 His visa application was rejected – it's possible that he made a mistake on the form. **might**
   _____

6 Perhaps Mika didn't read your email. **may**
   _____

6 Which responses are correct? Tick (✓) the correct box: a, b or both a and b.

1 I heard about this strange new chewing gum on the radio, and I think it was from Singapore.
   a It must have been from Singapore because chewing gum is illegal there.
   b It can't have been from Singapore because chewing gum is illegal there.
   a ☐   b ☐   both a and b ☐

2 Do you know who put that sign up yesterday?
   a It could have been Dino because he's responsible for safety here.
   b It can't have been Dino because he's on holiday this week.
   a ☐   b ☐   both a and b ☐

3 His application for an ID card has been refused.
   a Really? He might have filled in the form incorrectly.
   b Really? He must have filled in the form incorrectly.
   a ☐   b ☐   both a and b ☐

4 I have a photo of you driving a purple car, but I can't remember what year it was taken.
   a It must have been 1988 because I borrowed my mum's purple car that summer.
   b It can't have been 1987 because I didn't get my driving licence until 1988.
   a ☐   b ☐   both a and b ☐

5 I spoke to someone at Reception yesterday. A tall man with a moustache.
   a Ah! That must have been Gerhard. It sounds like him.
   b That might have been Gerhard because he has a moustache.
   a ☐   b ☐   both a and b ☐

BRING IT TOGETHER

7 Complete the text with the correct form of the words in brackets.

The year of the locust

As thousands of locusts descended on homes and villages in Senegal, Morocco, Mauritania and Egypt in 2004, people (1)_____ (must/be) terrified. Experts estimate that the swarm (2)_____ (may/be) the size of London and the swarm (3)_____ (might/include) up to 50 million insects. The only good news is that the locusts (4)_____ (could/cause) much more damage by entering the main food-producing areas of the countries. Fortunately, despite their 'swarm intelligence', they (5)_____ (can't/know) about the location of the main corn-producing fields of Senegal, or they would have devastated these areas. That (6)_____ (could/create) a huge food crisis across the continent.

As for how the swarm happened, scientists believe that good rains had created plenty of food for the locusts, and this (7)_____ (must/lead) to the sudden explosion in their numbers. Some people think that scientists (8)_____ (should/predict) the swarm, but others say that it was just a natural phenomenon. Either way, the swarm made 2004 'the year of the locust' for the victims of this terrifying plague.

Skills development

Functional language
Criticising

1 Complete the words.

> **A** Hello. Insurance Services.
>
> **B** Hello. I contacted your company weeks ago about a problem with water coming into our house. Since then, nobody has done anything. I want to know what's ⁽¹⁾g_____ on! My reference code is A91-0R.
>
> **A** Mr... Jackson. I have a record of calls from you on the 16th and 21st June.
>
> **B** That's right. The last time, a lady said the company would look into it. But the problem is, no one is telling us ⁽²⁾a_____! Have you any ⁽³⁾i_____ how much damage has been done to my house?
>
> **A** Well, we have arranged for someone to visit you within the next three weeks.
>
> **B** Three weeks! I'm afraid that just isn't good ⁽⁴⁾e_____! The water is damaging my house now! All I'm asking ⁽⁵⁾f_____ is someone to come and look at it.
>
> **A** And they will come, within three weeks.
>
> **B** So what are we ⁽⁶⁾s_____ to do now? Nothing? Three weeks is too long. You should have better systems in ⁽⁷⁾p_____. I've had problems with your company in the past. This isn't the ⁽⁸⁾f_____ time this has happened. I'd like to speak to your Complaints Department, please.
>
> **B** I'll put you through to Complaints now, Mr Jackson. Hold the line, please.

Listening
Inferring relationships

1 Look at the words for addressing people. Are they formal (F) or informal (I)?

1 darling   F / I   _____
2 dear   F / I   _____
3 madam   F / I   _____
4 officer   F / I   _____
5 sir   F / I   _____

2 a 🔊 7.2 Listen to four short conversations. Number the words in **1** in the order you hear them. There is one word that you don't need.

b Match conversations 1–4 to photos a–d.

a ☐   b ☐

c ☐   d ☐

3 Listen again. In which conversation (1–4)

1 has the speaker not understood something? _____
2 is the speaker trying to get to work? _____
3 has the speaker had this problem before? _____
4 does the speaker want to complain about something? _____

> **STRATEGY** When you listen to a conversation, think about the relationship between the speakers. Are they speaking formally or informally? How do they address each other? Making logical deductions about how the speakers know each other can help you understand what they are saying.

46

SKILLS 7

READING Skimming

1 a Look at the text. What kind of text is it? _____

b Read the text quickly. Who are the people 1–4? Match them to the words from the box.

| a fictional character   a journalist   a lawyer   a parent |

1 Gian Ettore Gassani _____   3 Friday _____
2 Mara O _____   4 Alain Elkann _____

2 Read the text again more slowly. Answer the questions.

Parents ordered to change child's name from Friday

By Chris Irvine

Italy's Court of Appeal has banned a couple from naming their son 'Friday' – Venerdi – because the name could expose the boy to ridicule. Named after the manservant of Daniel Defoe's famous novel *Robinson Crusoe*, the Cassation Court said the name was associated with being a servant. The judges also ordered the boy to be renamed Gregorio, named after the saint's day on which he was born.

The boy's parents, known only as Mara O and Roberto G, had said they should be free to name him as they pleased, and said they would continue to call the boy Friday, describing it as 'nice'. They even threatened to call their next child Mercoledi (Wednesday).

The verdict provoked mixed reaction across Italy. Gian Ettore Gassani of the Italian Association of Matrimonial Lawyers agreed with the ruling. He told an Italian news agency that Italian law mandated changes 'when the child's name is likely to limit social interaction and create insecurity'.

Italian journalist Alain Elkann argued that Friday was a good name, adding: 'It would have been different if they'd called him Friday the 13th.'

Friday joins an ever-growing list of banned names, which are arguably becoming more popular, rising because of the celebrity trend of unusual names for children.

In February, a judge in New Zealand made a young girl a ward of court so she could change her name from Talula Does The Hula From Hawaii. The judge said the name embarrassed the nine-year-old and could expose her to teasing.

Other names banned include twins called Fish and Chips, although Number 16 Bus Shelter was one of the more bizarre ones allowed. In New Zealand again, last year, a couple was banned from naming their baby 4Real, so they settled on Superman.

According to genealogy website findmypast.com, the UK has six boys named Gandalf, 29 Gazzas and even 36 Arsenals.

---

1 Why did the court reject the name 'Venerdi'?
_____

2 What name did Venerdi's parents say they would use for their child now?
_____

3 What name does a journalist suggest is worse than 'Venerdi'?
_____

4 Why are more and more people giving their children unusual names?
_____

5 Where else have unusual names been banned?
_____

6 Which unusual names have been permitted?
_____

STRATEGY When you read a difficult text for the first time, don't panic! Don't worry about understanding every word. Instead, read the text quickly and try to get a general understanding of it (the gist). Look for facts that will tell you the main subject of the text. Then read the text again more slowly.

8 Crime and punishment

Vocabulary
Crime

1 Read the descriptions. Write the name of the crimes.
1 The supermarket says that thousands of razors are stolen from their shelves every year. _____
2 Five people were almost killed when a car bomb was left near the police station. Police believe it was the work of a violent political group. _____
3 They stopped an elderly man while he was walking in the park. They showed him their knives and told him to give them all his money. _____
4 Someone went into our house while we were on holiday and stole the TV. _____
5 Some teenagers set fire to a school in their neighbourhood. _____
6 In the novel that I'm reading, a rich businessman is shot by a rival while he is sleeping. _____
7 Some kids broke all those windows for fun. _____
8 They received a note yesterday saying their 21-year-old son had been captured, and would not be released unless they paid $2 million. _____

2 Complete the text with the words and phrases from the box. There is one that you don't need.

| capital punishment | community service |
| corporal | fine | imprisonment | prison sentence |

Do existing punishments fit today's crimes?

The most serious penalty for a crime is (1)_____, the death penalty. In many countries, this is not a legal punishment and life (2)_____ is given instead for crimes like murder. However, despite its name, this may only mean a (3)_____ of 30 years. The reason is obvious. Too many people are in jail and it's expensive to keep them there. That's why governments prefer to tell people to pay a (4)_____ for minor offences like speeding, and why younger criminals can just be warned not to commit the offence again. Another punishment is (5)_____, where criminals have to work for free in their local area. Some people believe that these punishments are not serious enough and that (6)_____ punishment would be more effective because physical pain has more impact on people. Making the punishment fit the crime is a challenging issue faced by governments around the world. What do you think? Tell us your opinion by adding your comments below.

3 Choose the correct options to complete the sentences.
1 Someone's stolen my *apartment / trainers*!
2 My boss has been charged with *€10,000 / tax evasion*.
3 A boy at my school got arrested for *arson / some money*.
4 Don't do that! You're committing *a fine / a crime*!
5 Last week a man robbed my *mobile phone / parents' house*.
6 The company was found guilty of *illegal file sharing / life imprisonment*.

Scams

4 Complete the words.

A Have you ever been a victim of crime, Helmut?

B Well, yes. It was a scam really, not a big crime. I was on holiday and I wanted to hire a quad bike. The man asked for my ID card as security. I was a bit (1)n__ï____ really, because I trusted him.

A I suppose if you're a normal, (2)l__-ab__ __i__g citizen, you do trust people.

B Yes, exactly. When I returned the bike, the man said it was damaged and that he wouldn't give me back my ID card unless I paid a fine! We had a big argument and then this policeman appeared. Although I think he was a (3)b__g__ one, because he didn't listen to me at all. I couldn't be sure if he was real or not, but I wasn't going to argue with an (4)a__th__ __i__y f__ __u__e like that. I just paid, and the man got an extra $100.

A So the man renting quad bikes and the policeman were both (5)fr_____st__rs? Poor you. Well, put it down to experience. You won't be (6)t__ __en__n like that again.

48

On trial

5 Read the clues. Complete the crossword with words for the law.

Across
4 The ... accuse someone of a crime.
5 The ... speak for the person who is accused.
6 The ... are members of the public. They watch the trial and decide if the person is guilty or not.
7 A ... is someone who saw the crime and who tells the court what he/she saw.

Down
1 The ... is the person on trial. He/she has been accused of something.
2 The ... supervises the trial and makes the final decision about what punishment to give.
3 The ... is where the trial takes place.

VOCABULARY EXTENSION Police work

6 a Read the words and their definitions. Then complete the sentences with the words.

alibi (n) a piece of information that proves you did not do a crime because you were somewhere else
bail (n) before a trial, you can pay this money to the court to be free and not in prison
convicted (adj) found guilty of a crime by a court
DNA testing (n) a way of looking at someone's genetic code (DNA), e.g. from blood, to identify them
handcuffs (n) metal rings that the police put around someone's wrists when they arrest them
suspect (n) someone that the police think might have committed a crime

1 The police identified the murderer using _____.
2 The judge has agreed that you can pay _____ of €10,000 while you are waiting for your trial.
3 After the bank robbery, the police arrested one man, who they believe is the main _____.
4 Gordon's _____ is perfect. The robbery happened at 5 p.m., when he was on a plane over the Pacific.
5 The police put _____ on the mayor when they arrested him for corruption.
6 We bought a car that didn't work at all, and later we learnt we had bought it from a _____ fraudster!

b 🔊 8.1 Listen and check.

BRING IT TOGETHER

7 Complete the text with the words from the box. There is one word that you don't need.

bail   capital   commit   guilty   judge   jury   murder   prosecution   suspect   testing   witness

The CSI effect

The TV programme *CSI* is so successful that it's having an impact on real-life trials in the courtroom. This is called 'the *CSI* effect'. Many crimes can be solved based on normal evidence: if a (1)_____ saw the defendant (2)_____ the crime, for example. However, in the USA, the 12 person (3)_____ now expects to see forensic evidence as well. This is particularly true where the verdict could be (4)_____ punishment.

The problem is that when experts on *CSI* use DNA (5)_____, on blood and hair, for example, they say that it is completely trustworthy. When they investigate a crime, the TV characters quickly identify a (6)_____ by saying that his DNA matches DNA on the victim. But in real life, when people accuse someone of a crime such as (7)_____, the experts can only say DNA evidence could match. Their information is not really 100% accurate. However, today, people are suspicious of a case if it doesn't contain this type of evidence. It's difficult to believe someone is (8)_____ of a crime without seeing the same forensic evidence as on TV. Often, the (9)_____ says this is unnecessary. Nevertheless, the (10)_____ still have to provide this evidence, because that's what the people on the jury expect!

8

GRAMMAR
If sentences: imagined situations (1)

1 Complete the text with the correct form of the verb in brackets.

Luke Hartigan's crime blog... Police line-ups

If the police ⁽¹⁾_____ (suspect) you of a crime, one thing they would use to test your identity is a police line-up. If real life were like TV, everyone in the line-up ⁽²⁾_____ (look) more or less the same. But, in fact, they often look completely different! This is not a big problem. If the police ⁽³⁾_____ (put) the real criminal in the line-up, they would be identified correctly, after all. Or would they?

In fact, police line-ups are often used to test witnesses. If a police officer ⁽⁴⁾_____ (not/trust) a particular witness, they would show them two line-ups, the first one without the suspect. They ⁽⁵⁾_____ (only/show) them a second line-up if the witness didn't wrongly identify a suspect in the first one.

If the police only showed an untrustworthy witness one line-up, he or she ⁽⁶⁾_____ (just/choose) anyone. This is because a bad witness thinks the real suspect must be there! If a witness ⁽⁷⁾_____ (make) a false identification like this, an innocent person's life could be ruined. That is why the police need to control what happens in a line-up very carefully.

2 Correct the sentences. Tick (✓) two correct sentences.
1 If you were in the shop yesterday, would you have stopped the robbery?
2 If the criminals had go to prison, they wouldn't have committed any more crimes.
3 You might not have got that virus last week if you hadn't downloaded things from that file-sharing site.
4 There hadn't been so much crime last year, if there had been more police officers on the street.
5 If the jury saw this evidence in last year's trial, they could have found the man guilty of murder.
6 If there had been a lot of vandalism in the old days, everyone would have tried to stop it.
7 I was mugged! If I didn't hide my credit card in my socks, they would have taken that too!
8 If the flight hadn't been delayed, they would arrive five hours ago.

Wishes & regrets

3 a Order the words to make sentences.
a do the wish up would washing I he
_____
b would put online they wish I the lyrics
_____
c the Sunday opened only chemist on if
_____
d knew drive to how if I only
_____
e wish work I have I didn't to
_____
f started classes if the only later
_____

b Match 1–6 to responses a–f in **3a**.
1 You can't do this course because you have football practice at the same time. ____
2 Marco doesn't do much housework, does he? ____
3 There's no public transport to the festival so we can't get there. ____
4 I really can't understand the words of this song. ____
5 It's a shame you can't come to the beach with us. ____
6 I have a terrible headache, but I can't find any paracetamol. ____

4 Choose the correct options to complete the conversations.

1 A Rick got caught shoplifting at the local shop.
B Oh no! If only he *didn't become / hadn't become* friendly with the wrong crowd!

2 A Someone has vandalised my car again!
B If only we *had found out / could find out* who keeps doing it!

3 A I wish we *hadn't gone / could go* on that walk.
B I know. I can't believe that woman accused us of trespassing!

4 A The police have said that internet crime is rising all the time.
B If only they *had monitored / could monitor* everyone's computer to catch the fraudsters.

5 A Veronica's been accused of tax evasion.
B I know. She told me that she wishes she *had filled / filled* in her tax return more carefully.

If sentences: imagined situations (2), mixed time frames

5 Which sentences are correct? Tick (✓) the correct box: a, b or both a and b.

1. a If they had found the burglar guilty, they would have sent him to prison yesterday.
   b If they had found the burglar guilty, he would be in prison today.
   a ☐ b ☐ both a and b ☐

2. a If the woman had gone to prison, she wouldn't be doing community service now.
   b If the woman had gone to prison, she wouldn't have done community service now.
   a ☐ b ☐ both a and b ☐

3. a If I hadn't bought a paper yesterday, I wouldn't find out about the trial.
   b If I hadn't bought a paper yesterday, I wouldn't have found out about the trial.
   a ☐ b ☐ both a and b ☐

4. a We would still have capital punishment if the government hadn't changed the law in the 1960s.
   b We would still have had capital punishment if the government hadn't changed the law in the 1960s.
   a ☐ b ☐ both a and b ☐

5. a If we had caught the robber, he would be at the police station by now.
   b If we had caught the robber, he would have been at the police station by now.
   a ☐ b ☐ both a and b ☐

6. a You wouldn't have lost your money if you hadn't left your bag open.
   b You would have some money now if you hadn't left your bag open.
   a ☐ b ☐ both a and b ☐

7. a If last night's fire was caused by arson, there might still be evidence there.
   b If last night's fire had been caused by arson, there might still be evidence there.
   a ☐ b ☐ both a and b ☐

6 Rewrite the sentences, using the words in bold. Keep the same meaning.

1. I'm feeling ill so I didn't go to work this morning. **if/weren't**
   <u>If I weren't feeling ill, I would have gone to work this morning.</u>

2. Yolanda didn't get the job so she's still working in the same company. **if/wouldn't**
   _____

3. You don't watch television, so you didn't see the news about the kidnapping yesterday. **if/have**
   _____

4. I didn't cover up my PIN number. That's why the thief now has all my money. **if/had**
   _____

5. Monica missed the bus so she's walking home. **if/caught**
   _____

6. They parked their car in the wrong place and now they have a parking ticket. **if/wouldn't**
   _____

7. He visited the doctor. That's the reason why he's in hospital now. **hadn't/might**
   _____

8. We put security cameras in the shop so shoplifting isn't a big problem for us now. **if/be**
   _____

Bring it together

7 Complete the text with the correct form of the word(s) in brackets.

Miscarriage of justice

In the past, in Britain, criminals could be executed by hanging. This ended after a terrible miscarriage of justice.

Back in 1950, Timothy Evans was executed for the murder of his daughter after a very short trial. If the trial had been longer and more thorough, Evans ⁽¹⁾_____ (not/die) because in 1953 the police learnt that another person living at Evans's house had murdered other people. If the jury ⁽²⁾_____ (not/find) Evans guilty, the police might have stopped the real killer earlier. We all wish the police ⁽³⁾_____ (be) perfect. However, mistakes like this still happen today. Take the case of Norwegian Åge Vidar Fjell.

In 1990 he was found guilty of the murder of his neighbour. Twenty years later, the courts declared him innocent because of his mental state. Even if he ⁽⁴⁾_____ (be) at the crime scene, he could not have shot the victim. If only the court ⁽⁵⁾_____ (accept) this medical evidence back in 1990! Fortunately, Fjell was able to enjoy freedom again. If Norway ⁽⁶⁾_____ (have) the death penalty in 1990, he and other wrongly convicted people ⁽⁷⁾_____ (not/be) alive today.

Many of us wish that things like DNA testing ⁽⁸⁾_____ (provide) definite proof of someone's guilt. However, there are still problems, and for this reason, among others, the death penalty remains illegal in many countries.

Skills development

Functional language
Changing the subject

1 🔊 8.2 Listen to three conversations. Tick (✓) the topics that are mentioned.

> arson   burglary   court   dinner
> fraud   graffiti   judge   meeting
> money   vandalism

2 a Complete the sentences from the conversations in **1**.

1 No, sorry. _____ way, have you heard that she's leaving?
2 Next week apparently. _____ reminds me, she borrowed some money from me last week. I must get it back before she goes.
3 _____ , if you do see her, can you remind her that we're going for dinner this evening?
4 _____ trials, did you see the report about vandalism on the news last night?
5 _____ I forget, can you come in a bit early tomorrow? We've got a lot to cover.
6 All right. I'll try to be here by eight. _____ the subject, have you heard if there's a date for the arson court case?
7 _____ then, I should go. I don't want to miss my train.

b Listen again and check.

Listening
Listening for detail

1 a 🔊 8.3 Read Ben's notes about his journey. Listen to an announcement and answer the questions.

> Catch the 9.35 train from Canterbury to London.
> Arrive London Victoria 11.10.
> Change at London Victoria for 11.45 Brighton train.
> Arrive Brighton 12.40.

1 How will Ben travel to London now?
_____
2 What time will he leave?
_____
3 What time will he arrive in London?
_____
4 How does this affect his journey to Brighton?
_____

b Listen again. Correct six mistakes in the text below.

> Ladies and gentlemen, can I have your attention please? Due to looting on the railway line, trains will not be running from Canterbury to London this morning. Passengers for the 9.35 London service should wait in the ticket office for the replacement bus service. The buses will depart at about 10.15 and should arrive at London Waterloo at about 12.00. Trains from Canterbury to Dover are also affected. Please see signs in the station for more information. I'm very sorry for this change to your service, but the problem was only discovered this morning by the station staff. We hope that all services will be back to normal by early evening.

STRATEGY When you listen to a difficult audio, don't panic if you don't understand every word. Try to stay focused and listen for the key information you need.

SKILLS 8

WRITING A story

Things that go bump in the night

(1) It all happened when I was about 14 years old. My parents had gone out to an important dinner, and it was the first time that I had spent an evening alone at home. It was raining hard and it was very windy too, and I remember that I felt quite scared as I lay in bed. Eventually, I dropped off.

(2) Suddenly, I woke up. There was a strange noise downstairs! Silently, I lay in bed, listening. At first, I thought it was my parents coming home, but the clock said it was midnight, and I knew they wouldn't be back until two. Nevertheless, there was a steady tap, tap, tap. I was not alone!

(3) 'It must be burglars,' I thought. My heart was beating fast and I didn't know what to do. Even if I waited in bed, they might come upstairs. I needed to phone for help, but there were no mobiles in those days, and I needed to go to the living room to get to the phone. Slowly, I got up and I started to creep downstairs.

(4) The rain had stopped and the moon was shining through the windows. In its light, I saw a shadow on the kitchen floor. It had four legs and a tail moving from side to side. It did not look human. Happily, I ran downstairs towards the trespasser. It was a cat!

(5) Although we didn't have any pets, the kitchen door had a cat flap put in by the previous owners. The cat had got in, but then it couldn't get out, so it was trapped and it had to hit the flap with its paw to try to escape. That explained the noise. The poor animal was scared, so I quickly opened the door and it ran out into the night.

(6) The next morning when I told my parents about our visitor, we all thought it was quite funny, but it didn't feel like that at the time!

1 a Read the story quickly and answer the questions.
1 Why was the author on his own?
2 What sound did he hear?
3 Why did he get out of bed?
4 How had the weather changed?
5 How did he solve the problem?
6 How did his emotions about the incident change?

b Find words in the story that mean
1 fell asleep (*paragraph 1*).
2 regular, repeated (*paragraph 2*).
3 to move slowly and quietly (*paragraph 3*).
4 someone who has entered private property without permission (*paragraph 4*).
5 a special door to let a cat come in and out of a house (*paragraph 5*).
6 the foot of a cat, dog or similar animal (*paragraph 5*).

2 Complete the adverbs. Then check your answers in the text.
1 I felt quite scared as I lay in bed. E _ _ _ tu _ _ ly, I dropped off.
2 S _ _ d _ _ ly, I woke up. There was a strange noise downstairs!
3 S _ l _ _ tly, I lay in bed, listening.
4 S _ _ _ ly, I got up and I started to creep downstairs.
5 H _ _ p _ _ y, I ran downstairs towards the trespasser.
6 The poor animal was scared, so I q _ _ c _ _ y opened the door...

3 Write a story that ends with one of the sentences below.
1 It's a day that I'll remember my whole life.
2 That's how I met my best friend.
3 It was the best photo that I have ever taken.
4 I was absolutely furious!

STRATEGY When you write a story:
- begin with a phrase like *Once, One day* or *It all happened when* to set the scene, e.g. *It all happened when I was travelling around South America*.
- use the past continuous to describe what was happening when your story begins, e.g. your work, the weather.
- use a range of vocabulary to make your story interesting. Remember to use adverbs, e.g. *suddenly, amazingly, strangely* to describe *how* actions happened.

9 LUCK AND FORTUNE

VOCABULARY
Luck

1 Put the letters in brackets in the correct order to make words.

1 Some people believe in _____ (stydine) – that our future lives can only happen one way. But I believe _____ (sussecc) or _____ (afeluri) depends on how hard you work.
2 On New Year's Eve in Italy, some people serve lentils to represent _____ (sopiprerty) because lentils look like coins.
3 My partner and I met in the supermarket by _____ (cachen). I think it was _____ (tefa) – we were meant to be together!
4 People say that health, _____ (ehlawt) and happiness are the key to a good life, but I think health and happiness are much more important than money!
5 Last year I had the good _____ (nutrefo) to be offered a new job. I've never been happier!

2 Complete the phrases with *luck*.

1 I hoped I'd win the card game but n __ s __ __ __ l __ __ __ . Erik beat me again!
2 I have to do a big presentation at work tomorrow – w __ __ __ me l __ __ __ !
3 OK, you can go to the party, but don't p __ __ __ y __ __ __ l __ __ __ . Make sure you're home by midnight.
4 I left my scarf on the train, but w __ __ __ a __ __ l __ __ __ , someone will have handed it in to the lost property office.
5 All of my exams went well except for the last one. I guess I had r __ __ o __ __ of l __ __ __ .
6 I just found €10 inside this library book – what a s __ __ __ __ __ o __ l __ __ __ !

Sport

3 Match 1–7 to a–g.

1 We wanted to go running today, but
2 Shelia has lost her racquet, but
3 Ildiko has some knee pads for ice hockey, but
4 To join the baseball team, everyone needs a helmet and
5 We had great seats for the football match –
6 There's a lot of chlorine in the pool so
7 I don't own any golf clubs –

a it's probably next to the court where she last used it.
b we sat right next to the pitch!
c the track's closed.
d I rent them when I'm at the course.
e it's best to wear goggles and a cap.
f their own bat.
g she needs to borrow some skates to play.

Verb collocations

4 Choose the correct options to complete the conversations.

1 A I'm running *down / low* on cash.
  B There's a cash machine round the corner. You can get some money there.

2 A We're arranging a conference and we need to find hotel rooms for 50 guests!
  B Don't worry, I'll *make / take* care of it for you. I know lots of hotels.

3 A This washing machine is useless! It never works properly.
  B Why don't you *get / have* rid of it and buy a new one?

4 A I'll be late home this evening.
  B Well, bear in *head / mind* that your grandparents are visiting tonight. They want to see you, too.

5 A Did you have a good time in India? Did you see any tigers?
  B Yes, we caught *sight / view* of one for a moment, but then it disappeared into the jungle. They're quite shy, really.

6 A Have you got Jeremy's phone number?
  B No, I haven't. I've kind of *lost / missed* touch with him.

54

VOCABULARY EXTENSION
Sport collocations

5 a Match sport collocations a–h to photos 1–8.

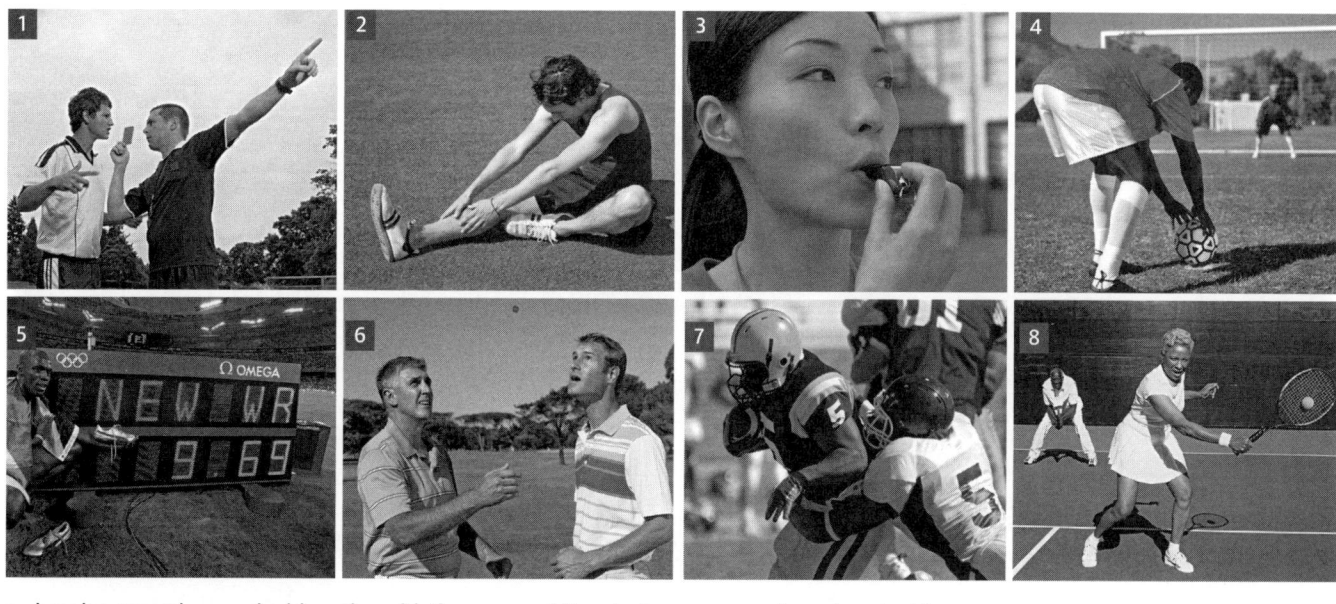

a break a record
b blow the whistle
c hit a shot
d make a tackle
e send off (a player)
f toss a coin
g take a penalty
h warm up

b 9.1 Listen and check.

6 Complete the two emails with the correct form of the collocations from 5a.

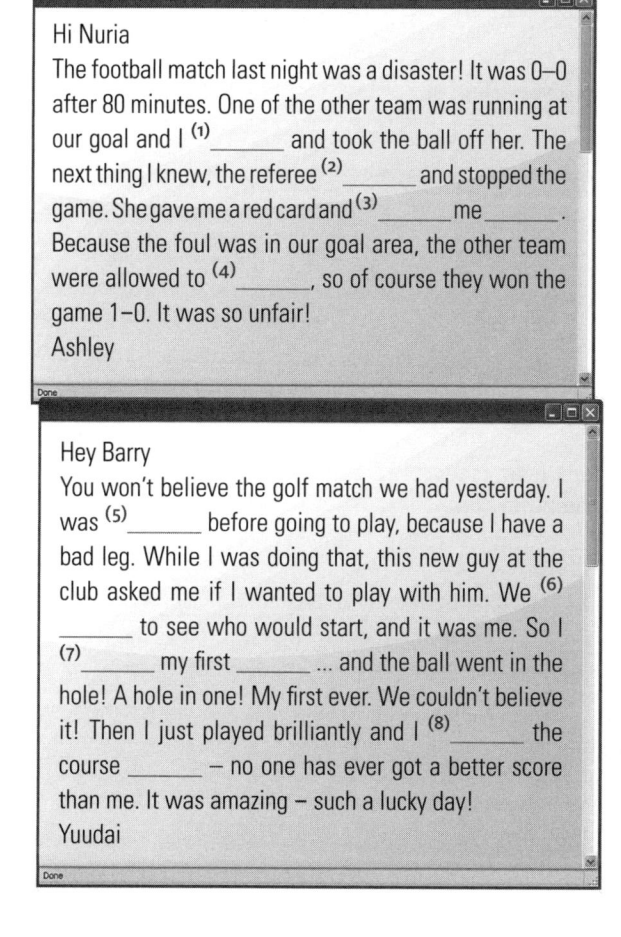

Hi Nuria
The football match last night was a disaster! It was 0–0 after 80 minutes. One of the other team was running at our goal and I ⁽¹⁾_____ and took the ball off her. The next thing I knew, the referee ⁽²⁾_____ and stopped the game. She gave me a red card and ⁽³⁾_____ me _____. Because the foul was in our goal area, the other team were allowed to ⁽⁴⁾_____, so of course they won the game 1–0. It was so unfair!
Ashley

Hey Barry
You won't believe the golf match we had yesterday. I was ⁽⁵⁾_____ before going to play, because I have a bad leg. While I was doing that, this new guy at the club asked me if I wanted to play with him. We ⁽⁶⁾_____ to see who would start, and it was me. So I ⁽⁷⁾_____ my first _____ ... and the ball went in the hole! A hole in one! My first ever. We couldn't believe it! Then I just played brilliantly and I ⁽⁸⁾_____ the course _____ – no one has ever got a better score than me. It was amazing – such a lucky day!
Yuudai

BRING IT TOGETHER

7 Put the letters in brackets in the correct order to complete the text.

In most jobs, ⁽¹⁾_____ (cussces) doesn't come from luck, but sport is different. Hitting a lucky ⁽²⁾_____ (host) in tennis or making a last-minute ⁽³⁾_____ (ketlac) in football could mean the difference between winning and losing. This means that athletes the world over are fond of carrying lucky charms to ensure their good ⁽⁴⁾_____ (tournef). One of the most famous was basketball player Michael Jordan, who always wore his lucky college shorts underneath his team shorts! He did this for every NBA game he played, hoping they would bring him a ⁽⁵⁾_____ (oktrse) of luck that would win the match.
Scientists in Germany wanted to find out whether using lucky charms could really change your ⁽⁶⁾_____ (sdytnei). They gave golfers a 'lucky' ball and a normal ball. All the players used the same ⁽⁷⁾_____ (bulcs), but they all played better with the lucky ball. The scientists' explanation is that when people believe in lucky symbols, it gives them confidence. When sports people are confident, they play better and have a better ⁽⁸⁾_____ (echanc) of becoming winners. So this really works!
Michael Jordan is a classic example. His lucky shorts helped him avoid bad luck on the basketball ⁽⁹⁾_____ (cruto) – he ⁽¹⁰⁾_____ (rekbo) the record for the highest season average score, and became one of the most successful players in history.

9

GRAMMAR
Adding emphasis: cleft sentences with *is*

1 Complete the words to make cleft sentences.

Morning rituals

Jackie OK everyone. Today's question is 'what's your morning ritual like?' For example, (1) w_____ I love to do i_____ read the paper on my way to work. Most people don't enjoy commuting, but I find it quite relaxing.

Anwar The (2) t_____ t_____ I always do is drink a strong, black coffee. That's a ritual here in Jordan! The (3) p_____ t_____ I buy it from is a friend of mine, so we always have a chat too (normally about football!).

Letícia I live in Rio and every morning I go for a run at 6 a.m. The (4) r_____ w_____ I go so early is that it's nice and cool at that time of day. Also, there aren't many people about – (5) i_____ the peace and quiet t_____ really clears my head.

Bruce The first (6) t_____ t_____ I do in the morning is go to bed! I'm a security guard and I work night shifts. But before I go to sleep, I always have a meal with my kids – they eat breakfast, but for me it's more like an evening meal!

Making comparisons

3 Choose the correct options to complete the sentences.
1. That was the *more / most* difficult tennis match I've ever played!
2. Some athletes believe that training *hard and harder / harder and harder* will guarantee success.
3. The *quicker / quickly* you drive, the faster we'll arrive.
4. I think she is the *best / better* swimmer I've ever trained.
5. The harder you train, the *more successful / most successful* you will be.
6. Tickets for sports events are becoming *more and more / more and most* expensive.

2 a Complete the second sentence so that it means the same as the first sentence.
1. I chose this profession because I love performing.
   The reason why _____
2. Making people laugh is the best thing about this job.
   What I really love about this job _____
3. I also like travelling to different places with the show.
   Another thing _____
4. I don't like my costume. It's not very comfortable.
   The thing _____
5. Seeing my friends in the audience makes me feel anxious.
   It's _____
6. Strangely, my girlfriend makes me the most nervous!
   Strangely, the person _____

b Look at photos a–c. Which job does the person in **2a** do?

4 Complete the sentences with the correct form of the words in brackets. You may need to add extra words.
1. Emmanuel is _____ athlete we've ever had in this school. (good)
2. Our swimming team is terrible – and we're getting _____ and _____ all the time! (bad)
3. That was _____ football match I've ever seen! Our team was awful! (disappointing)
4. _____ I spend in the gym, _____ I get! (long, hungry)
5. I only started playing golf two months ago. But I'm feeling _____ and _____ each time I play. (confident)
6. Brendon is _____ baseball fan I've ever met – he never misses a game! (dedicated)
7. _____ you skate, _____ it becomes. You really must wear a helmet. (fast, dangerous)
8. _____ I've ever run is 12 kilometres. I was exhausted afterwards! (far)

Modifying comparisons

5 Complete the words in the online interview.

> Today's online chat is with competitions guru Mia Leung. Join us live from 12.00 CET.
>
> **I** Mia, you've won over 200 competitions. How?
>
> **M** It's not that I'm a ⁽¹⁾l _ _ luckier than other people, but I do have some strategies for people who want to become a ⁽²⁾b _ _ better at winning competitions.
>
> **I** Tell us more.
>
> **M** If you enter lots of competitions, you are ⁽³⁾f _ _ more likely to win something. And don't forget competitions by local businesses. Sometimes only a few people enter them so your chance of winning is ⁽⁴⁾m _ _ _ higher than in other competitions. You're ⁽⁵⁾n _ _ _ _ _ _ near as likely to win a national competition – especially one for a big prize.
>
> **I** OK.
>
> **M** In national competitions, you often have to answer a question in 25 words. The competition judges see hundreds of sentences, so if your one is funny, you have a ⁽⁶⁾s _ _ _ _ _ _ _ better chance of winning. If you can't think of anything funny then make your entry rhyme. That's ⁽⁷⁾j _ _ _ as good as a joke because the judges can remember it.
>
> **I** Any other advice?
>
> **M** Yes. Sometimes you can enter many times. I once won a holiday like that – it's not ⁽⁸⁾n _ _ _ _ _ _ as difficult as you think!

6 Rewrite the sentences using the words in bold. Keep the same meaning.

1. Playing football is easier than playing golf. **not / nearly**
   Playing football is not nearly as hard as playing golf.

2. Cricket bats and tennis racquets are equally expensive. **just / expensive**

3. Watching golf is not nearly as interesting as watching athletics. **nowhere / interesting**

4. My new helmet is slightly bigger than my old one. **not / quite**

5. Yellow golf balls are as easy to see as white ones. **any / easier**

6. Volleyball isn't nearly as popular as football. **far / more**

7. Our seats in the stadium aren't quite as good as your ones. **bit / worse**

8. The other players on the team are a little fitter than us. **quite / as**

9. My racquet was cheap, but it wasn't as cheap as my mum's. **slightly / mine**

BRING IT TOGETHER

7 Choose the correct options to complete the text.

The end of records?

The long jump competition in the 1991 World Championships in Tokyo was the ⁽¹⁾*greater / greatest* competition I've ever seen. The thing ⁽²⁾*that / what* made it special was the rivalry between Carl Lewis and Mike Powell. These athletes were ⁽³⁾*slightly / far* better than all of the others in the competition – no one else could jump ⁽⁴⁾*near / nearly* as far as them. Lewis jumped an amazing 8.91 metres but then Powell jumped ⁽⁵⁾*slight / slightly* further – 8.95 metres, to break the world record and win the gold medal. Powell's world record has been unbeaten for over 20 years.

In the past, records were broken all the time. In the 1960s the long jump record was broken nine times. This was because of improving sports science. The ⁽⁶⁾*fit / fitter* the athletes became, the better they performed. However, some scientists believe we're now reaching the end of sports records. What they say ⁽⁷⁾*it's / is* that there's a limit to how much a human being can run or jump, and they think that today's athletes are already at that limit.

This phenomenon is ⁽⁸⁾*just / quite* as common in women's sports as in men's. In the women's 1500 metres the ⁽⁹⁾*faster / fastest* time ever recorded is 3:50.46, a record set by China's Qu Yunxia in 1993. The reason ⁽¹⁰⁾*why / who* Qu's record remains the fastest and Powell's record remains the longest is because they may be the absolute human maximum for those events.

Skills development

Functional language
Arguing and making concessions

1 Choose the correct options to complete the underlined phrases.

1. A Matteo's really good at speaking in public, isn't he?
   B What? You must be *laughing / joking*! I find his speeches really boring!

2. A I've told you a thousand times that we can't go to the match next week.
   B Don't *exaggerate / overestimate*. I forgot that you told me, OK?

3. A I'd like to spend the rest of the budget on building a skate park.
   B I'm not sure *I agree / I'm agreeing* with you there. How many people will use it?

4. A You want to get a new set of golf clubs? That'll cost a fortune!
   B I take your *opinion / point*, but it'll be worth it. It will really improve my game.

5. A Getting into the film industry is impossible if your family isn't in the business.
   B Oh, come *on / off*! Lots of people manage to get into it without knowing anyone.

6. A A lot of actors refuse to go on stage unless they have their lucky charm with them.
   B That may be the *case / way*, but I'm sure it doesn't make any difference to their performance.

7. A The best athletes are the most dedicated, that's all. They just train harder than their opponents.
   B I *propose / suppose* you're right, but don't you think some athletes are just naturally better than the rest?

8. A Isn't Carla a bit too old to have that lucky teddy? She's nearly nine.
   B I understand *what / that* you're saying, but she'd be so upset if I took it away.

2 Complete the chart using the underlined phrases from **1**.

Disagreeing	Making concessions

Listening Identifying emotion

1 a 9.2 Listen to four conversations. Tick (✓) if one of the speakers is angry. Cross (✗) if neither speaker is angry.

Conversation 1 ☐   Conversation 2 ☐
Conversation 3 ☐   Conversation 4 ☐

b Listen again and choose the correct answer a, b or c.

Conversation 1
1. What does the man not have?
   a goggles   b a hat   c a towel
2. What happens at the end of the conversation?
   a The man buys the thing that he needs.
   b The man goes home to get the thing that he needs.
   c The man leaves the swimming pool and doesn't come back.

Conversation 2
3. Which of these things does the person offer Mariam?
   a cheap telephone calls   b satellite television
   c a Wi-Fi connection
4. How many calls like this has Mariam had today?
   a one   b three   c five

Conversation 3
5. Why didn't Suresh win any money?
   a He lost his lottery ticket.
   b He changed his lottery numbers.
   c He forgot to buy a lottery ticket.
6. What did Suresh buy yesterday?
   a a lottery ticket   b a card   c a lucky charm

Conversation 4
7. Where was Joe's skateboard stolen?
   a in the road   b at school
   c in the sports centre
8. How did Joe get the skateboard?
   a It was a present.   b It was a prize.
   c He bought it with money from his job.

> **Strategy** When you listen, think carefully about how the speakers sound. Are they happy, angry or upset? Identifying a speaker's emotion can help you understand what they're saying.

SKILLS 9

READING Scanning

1 a Each question 1–5 has a word in bold. Find this word in the text to answer the question. Do not read the whole text.

1 How many things does a **British** bride need on her wedding day?
_____

2 What do a Tajik bride and groom eat during the wedding **ceremony**?
_____

3 What **ritual** does the bride do after the wedding?
_____

4 What is **plov**?
_____

5 Why is a **government** official at the wedding?
_____

b Read the whole text again. Have these parts of the Tajik wedding ceremony changed recently? Write a tick (✓) for yes or a cross (✗) for no.

1 The ritual that happens when the guests arrive. ☐
2 The clothing that the bride wears. ☐
3 The preparation of dough by the bride. ☐
4 The number of guests at the wedding. ☐
5 The number of courses at the wedding. ☐
6 The recipe of *plov*. ☐
7 The length of the wedding. ☐
8 The cost of the wedding. ☐

'Something old, something new'

'Something old, something new, something borrowed, something blue' is one of the most famous phrases in the English language, representing the four things that every British bride needs for luck on her wedding day. It's a tradition that goes back centuries, as weddings remain an unchanging part of society. Weddings in other parts of the world, like Tajikistan, are just as traditional, although change is in the air.

The first thing that happens in a Tajik wedding is the arrival of the guests, who have their hands washed by a member of the family in the traditional way. The bride will appear later, with her face hidden beneath a veil. Then she will join the groom for the ceremony. Once they have made their promises, the couple drink water and eat a little meat with a pancake to confirm the marriage.

Afterwards, the bride says farewell to her family and is escorted to her new home, where she performs an ancient ritual. She takes oil and flour and mixes them to make dough, to show that she is an able cook. She even performs this simple act in her wedding dress. Meanwhile, outside, the guests enjoy a huge festival of music and dance.

From the outside, this event seems almost timeless, but in fact, marriages in Tajikistan are changing. There are hard times across the country, and the less work there is available, the harder it is to pay for weddings of this size. In the past, the family might have had to spend an enormous amount of money to pay for the big day. To solve the problem, the government has taken a stand.

In 2011, they introduced a series of new rules. A wedding can have a maximum of 150 guests, and the feast eaten by the guests must only be three hours long. The family are also only allowed to serve a single course. Most people cook plov, the traditional dish of Tajikistan, as the sole dish of the day. This delicious dish is a mixture of lamb, rice and vegetables.

These restrictions have been a huge departure from the traditional weddings, which were once among the longest in the world, with festivities continuing for over a week. To enforce the law, there is one extra person attending, a government representative who ensures that the rules are being followed. So far, it seems to have been a success, and it's surely good news for the parents of Tajikistan, who no longer fear being bankrupted by celebrations.

STRATEGY You don't always need to read an entire text to get the information that you need. If you are looking for particular information, scan over the text quickly for key words.

PROGRESS TEST 3

GRAMMAR & VOCABULARY
(25 points)

1 Complete each sentence with one word in each gap (*isn't*, etc. = one word). *(5 points)*

0 The harder you train, _the_ easier it will be to run the marathon.
1 My legs are really hurting. I _____ have spent so long in the gym yesterday.
2 You _____ have left your trainers at the track, Elnaz. You were wearing them when we left there!
3 Alex's running is improving all the time – he's getting faster and _____ .
4 The _____ that I like about running is that you don't need any expensive equipment.
5 _____ I want to know is why the race was cancelled.

2 Complete the sentences with the correct form of the word in brackets. *(5 points)*

0 Gary's not here. He _must have gone_ (go) home early today.
1 If I had seen you yesterday, I _____ (invite) you to the office party.
2 If I'd passed all my exams, I _____ (be) at university now.
3 I wish I _____ (have) a job. I hate being here in the job centre.
4 I sent my boss a really angry email, and then he sacked me. If only I _____ (do) that!
5 If I _____ (have) a car, I wouldn't be able to drive to work.

3 a Choose the correct options to complete the sentences. *(5 points)*

0 Our line manager was charged with *money / tax* evasion. No one was surprised, as we all thought he was a _dishonest_ (honest) man.
1 You can trust David to *take / have* care of any problems with the project. He's very _____ (rely).
2 In some countries, *capital / death* punishment is used as a penalty for murder. In other places, this punishment has been made _____ (legal).
3 The tour guide seemed really _____ (trust). We were completely *taken / pulled* in by her act – we couldn't believe it when we found out that she'd stolen our wallets!
4 I was really _____ (care) when I filled in my tax *back / return*. Now I have to do it again, because I made so many mistakes!
5 Three teenagers were arrested *for / of* vandalism on the railway line. The police said their behaviour was extremely _____ (responsible), because they could have caused a crash.

b Complete the gaps with the correct form of the words in brackets. Add a prefix or suffix. *(5 points)*

4 Complete the sentences with the correct form of words from the box. There is one word that you don't need. *(5 points)*

| crew | club | horde | jury |
| stroke | ~~success~~ | swarm | |

0 Her business has been a great _success_ .
1 Don't go outside! There's a _____ of bees in the garden!
2 My mum has to go to court next month because she's going to be on the _____ for a trial.
3 We won $600 in the lottery last year – it was a real _____ of luck.
4 My sister's going to work on the _____ of a cruise ship for six months.
5 We bought Julia some new golf _____ for her birthday.

READING *(25 points)*

1 Read the text on page 61 quickly. What kind of text is it? *(3 points)*
a factual report ☐   b magazine article ☐
c travel guide ☐

2 a Which five countries are mentioned in the text? *(5 points)*

a _____ _____   b _____ _____
c _____ _____   d _____ _____
e _____ _____

b Match the numbers in the box to the countries in **2a**. One country matches two numbers. *(5 points)*

| 8 | 13 | 17 | 39 | 49 |

3 Answer the questions. *(12 points)*

1 What part of his vehicle did the man change in Afghanistan?
_____
2 How do the Afghan police feel about this kind of crime?
_____
3 What is missing from many apartment blocks in America?
_____
4 Why does the author not explain why 13 and 17 are unlucky?
_____
5 Which number is considered lucky because of how it is written?
_____
6 Why did the Beijing Olympics start on 8 August?
_____

60

TEST 3

Lucky for some...

1 I had been working in Afghanistan for a couple of months when, one day, I found my next-door neighbour painting his car number plate. He was calmly removing 39 from the end of it by changing them from black to white. When I asked him whether it was illegal, he just told me it was alright 'because the police understand'. It seems that the number 39 is very unlucky in his country, and people feel ashamed to be associated with it.

2 In those circumstances, maybe it's not unreasonable to change your car number plate. This sort of thing happens all over the world. In the States many apartment blocks don't have a thirteenth floor because it's considered unlucky! It may seem foolish and superstitious, but it does make business sense. If people won't buy an apartment on the thirteenth floor, there's no reason to have one!

3 Funnily enough, in Italy, it's the number 17 that you need to be careful about! So there isn't a seat row with that number on Alitalia planes, for example. Just like lucky rituals, it's hard to say where these superstitions come from – there are so many theories, it would be impossible for me to explain them all here!

4 In Asia, these superstitions are often related to language. In Japan, you're very unlikely to find a hotel room with the number 49 because those numbers together sound like the word for death. People don't want to think about such negative subjects while they're on holiday.

5 On the other hand, they love the number eight, because its Japanese character shows two expanding lines. The idea is that they mean 'prosperity'. Across the sea in China, people also think of this number as the key to wealth and success. It's so popular that organisers decided to open the Beijing Olympics at 8 a.m. on 8 August, 2008. Perhaps the number really is lucky, because they were one of the best Olympics in history!

LISTENING (25 points)

1 🔊 T3 Listen to a radio news report. Which crimes does the presenter talk about? Number the crimes 1–5. There is one crime that you don't need. *(5 points)*

arson ☐   murder ☐
burglary ☐   trespassing ☐
illegal file sharing ☐   vandalism ☐

2 Listen again. Answer the questions. *(20 points)*

0 What were the protestors trying to enter?
   A nuclear power station.

1 How old were the protestors?
   _____

2 When were the protesters allowed to go home?
   _____

3 What was damaged in New Town?
   _____

4 What punishment can people now get for this kind of crime?
   _____

5 How many warnings do people get before their internet service is stopped?
   _____

6 How many computers have already been disconnected?
   _____

7 How much will the repairs at Good Hope High School cost?
   _____

8 Who was responsible for starting the fire?
   _____

9 What job did Bruce Twining use to do?
   _____

10 What punishment did Roger Churchill receive?
   _____

WRITING (25 points)

1 Complete the words in the blog post. *(5 points)*

| Home | Blog | Links | Photos | About | Contact |

When football fans get together at the stadium, they turn into a mob. Their behaviour can become irresponsible, disrespectful and even violent – they often cause damage and disruption in the local area. In (1)a _ _ _ _ _ _ n , they give the sport a bad reputation. Of (2)c _ _ _ _ _ , I'm not saying that the people who go to football matches behave like this every day. There's no (3)q _ _ _ _ _ _ that their actions change because they're part of a large group of people: psychologists have (4)f _ _ _ d that people behave differently when they're in a crowd. I couldn't (5)a _ _ _ _ more with people who say that punishments for this behaviour should be tougher. In my opinion, 'herd mentality' isn't an excuse.

posted by CarlosV at 13.59

2 Write a blog post. Reply to the post in **1**, giving your opinion. *(20 points)*

61

10 VALUE FOR MONEY

Vocabulary
Phrasal verbs about money

1 Complete the online chat with the correct form of the phrasal verbs from the box.

> cut back   fork out   get by   pay off
> rip off   run out of   save up   take out

> **Today's online chat is with retail expert Ann Dobson. Join us live from 4 p.m. GMT.**
>
> **I** Many families find it difficult to (1)_____ financially. How can people (2)_____ on their spending to reduce their supermarket bill?
>
> **A** Well, many people go shopping when they (3)_____ something essential like flour. This is a bad idea if you haven't eaten. Never go to the supermarket hungry, or you'll (4)_____ on lots of things you don't really need.
>
> **I** So do supermarkets (5)_____ their customers – make them pay more than the fair price?
>
> **A** Not really, but they have little tricks to encourage people to buy more.
>
> **I** I see.
>
> **A** Sometimes supermarkets help, though. With a store card, you get points every time you shop. If you (6)_____ your points, you can get bargains in the future.
>
> **I** And what about a shopping list?
>
> **A** A list is essential. Plan your shopping before going to the supermarket, then only buy things on your list. Otherwise there are so many things to buy – you don't want to (7)_____ a loan just to pay for your weekly food shopping! Another tip: leave cards at home. I knew one man who had trouble (8)_____ his credit card bills every month. He started only taking cash to the supermarket, to stop overspending.
>
> **I** Ann, thanks for your advice!

Materials

2 Find 14 materials in the word search.

V	P	O	L	Y	E	S	T	E	R
A	L	E	A	T	H	E	R	C	U
L	A	S	T	E	E	L	Z	A	B
U	S	Q	S	W	O	O	L	R	B
M	T	D	I	K	Z	B	J	D	E
I	I	J	L	Q	J	K	W	B	R
N	C	L	K	F	G	D	A	O	N
I	V	B	V	K	Z	V	X	A	R
U	J	N	Y	L	O	N	Q	R	P
M	A	H	O	G	A	N	Y	D	I
F	U	H	S	C	O	T	T	O	N
A	M	K	T	Y	S	L	D	I	E

3 Choose the correct options to complete the sentences.
1. *Aluminium / Mahogany* is a very useful metal.
2. Scientists invented *nylon / silk* in the twentieth century.
3. I always wear *rubber / wool* gloves when I do the washing-up.
4. I prefer clothes that are made from natural fibres like *polyester / cotton*.
5. My kids love drawing with *cardboard / wax* crayons.
6. Sarah always buys *leather / plastic* shoes because she doesn't want to wear animal products.
7. *Steel / Pine* is often used in large building projects, because it's very strong.

Adjective order

4 Put the adjectives in brackets in the right order to complete the adverts. Do you ever write adverts like these?

(1)_____ (black / stylish / leather) jacket for sale. Size 38. Contact me on ep23@email.com.

FOR SALE – (2)_____ (round / dining / large / pine) table. Excellent condition!

Now available – a set of (3)_____ (rare / American / old) postcards, some very valuable. Call 5780-192 for more info.

(4)_____ (Italian / mountain / second-hand) bike for sale, only £49. A real bargain!

62

Business & finance

5 Match 1–5 to a–e to make questions.
1. How did you get the capital ___
2. When did you start running ___
3. Did you get a grant ___
4. What service ___
5. What are your company's ___

a do you provide?
b to start the business?
c day-to-day expenses?
d from the government?
e your business?

6 a Read the interview with a businesswoman. Complete a–e with the questions from **5**.

Today I'm talking to Mette Lund, successful businesswoman and company owner.

(a) _____

I started the business when I was 19 because I needed to pay my (1)_____ through college. I didn't want to get into (2)_____ if I could avoid it!

(b) _____

We help people and companies who want to recycle old technology equipment. The metals used in things like mobile phones can be worth a lot of money.

(c) _____

At first, I used my savings – I started with about $400! Later, I persuaded local companies to (3)_____ in the business.

(d) _____

No, we didn't. We did borrow money from the bank, though. I'm starting to repay that (4)_____ now that the company is making a (5)_____ . In the first few years, we didn't make any money – we just had enough to (6)_____ our running costs.

(e) _____

Renting our office space, and staff salaries. We try to give our employees good (7)_____ and we regularly send them on training courses.

Well thanks very much, Mette. We hope the business continues to grow!

b Complete 1–7 with words from the box. There is one word that you don't need.

benefits   cover   debt   invest
loan   profit   return   way

Vocabulary extension
Further materials

7 a Match the objects in the box to materials 1–6. Some objects match more than one material.

cup   floor   statue   tile   wire

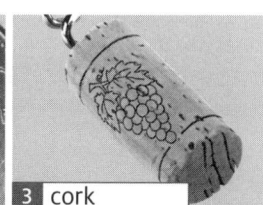

1 concrete
2 copper
3 cork
4 marble
5 ceramic
6 polystyrene

b Can you think of any other objects which are made with these materials?

8 a Complete the sentences with a material from **7a**.
1. A lot of food and drink packaging is made of _____ .
2. The old temple in the town centre is made of beautiful white _____ .
3. _____ is often used to make electricity cables.
4. Bottles of wine or oil often have tops made of _____ .
5. There are too many ugly grey _____ buildings in this city.
6. The walls of the villa are decorated with painted _____ tiles.

b 🔊 10.1 Listen and check.

Bring it together

9 Choose the correct options to complete the text.

→→ Save! Save! Save! ←←

With our top money-saving tips, you'll never be ripped (1)*off / up*!

Tip #1 Sign up for websites like Groupon, which offers discounts in local shops and restaurants. They (2)*provide / perform* a great service for people who want to save money.

Tip #2 Think carefully before you fork (3)*up / out* on (4)*big expensive / expensive big* purchases like furniture or a piece of technology. If you want a new (5)*pine / polystyrene* dining table, or the (6)*digital latest / latest digital* camera, find out when the shops will be having their next sale. Stores often lower their prices after big national holidays.

Tip #3 If you're trying to save (7)*back / up* some money, be prepared to change your bank account quite regularly. This can help you to get the highest (8)*repay / return* on the money you invest.

If you have a great money-saving tip, share it here! Write a comment

10

GRAMMAR
Either... or/neither... nor

1 Choose the correct options to complete the text.

Must go Moscow

Moscow is a real treat for architecture fans. If you go on a trip to the Russian capital, you can (1)*either / or* spend your time looking at modern buildings, (2)*and / or* medieval buildings from the country's past. Red Square in the centre is a perfect place to start your trip. You can (3)*either / neither* go shopping in the GUM superstore on one side of the square, (4)*or / nor* visit The Kremlin and its museums on the other side. Tourists always go to this area, but for me, (5)*either / neither* building is as impressive as the 'Seven Sisters'. These are a group of buildings that were built from 1947 to 1953. One of the most famous is the Russian Foreign Ministry building. Unfortunately, you can (6)*either / neither* go inside it (7)*nor / or* take a guided tour. You just have to take photographs outside. However, one of the group is the Hotel Leningradskaya. You can (8)*either / neither* spend the night here (9)*or / nor* just have a meal in its beautiful restaurant. Be careful though – (10)*either / neither* one is cheap, and this is not an option for the budget traveller!

2 Match comments 1–6 to a–f.

1 The hotel was terrible! It was neither near the beach ___
2 What are you doing for the party? You can either bring some snacks ___
3 Someone is going to be the new manager. It's either going to me ___
4 You can either pay in cash ___
5 I was very upset with the course. The teachers were neither friendly ___
6 The city wasn't very interesting. It had neither a museum ___

a nor in the centre of the town.
b or Griselda Vilchez.
c nor an art gallery.
d or by credit card.
e nor well-prepared.
f or some paper plates and polystyrene cups.

3 Complete the comments from a customer survey using the words in brackets. Remember to use the correct form of the verbs.

> Do you ever use our online shopping service? How can we improve it? We'd love to hear your ideas!

I usually find that (1)_____ the website (2)_____ my computer (3)_____ while I'm trying to pay! So I prefer to buy things in the store.
(crash / either / or)

I think the online service works really well. It's great that I can (4)_____ online (5)_____ the store in the city centre.
(shop / or / visit / either)

No, I never shop online. In my opinion, it's (6)_____ quicker, (7)_____ easier! There always seem to be problems.
(nor / neither)

I think you need to keep more products in stock. Sometimes (8)_____ the online shop (9)_____ your branches in town (10)_____ the things I'm looking for!
(have / neither / nor)

Articles

4 Complete the sentences with *a*, *an*, *the* or Ø (= no article).

1 There was _____ letter for you this morning. _____ envelope said it was from Chile.
2 Who was _____ man you met in _____ Hotel Suiza?
3 Health experts warn people that _____ fruit juice contains a lot of _____ sugar.
4 You look exhausted. You need to take _____ holiday or _____ day off or something.
5 You can stay in _____ bedroom at the top of the house. It's my daughter's, but she's away at _____ university at the moment.
6 I saw _____ amazing silk shirt this morning. It was _____ coolest shirt that I've ever seen.
7 I want to get _____ cat, but my parents don't like _____ pets.
8 _____ Indus river begins in _____ Himalayas.

5 Which sentences are correct? Tick (✓) the correct box: a, b or both a and b.

1. a Dad's gone to the shops to buy newspaper.
   b Dad's in the living room reading the newspaper.
   a ☐   b ☐   both a and b ☐

2. a There's something wrong with my ankle. It hurts.
   b The doctor needs to look at the ankle that's hurting you.
   a ☐   b ☐   both a and b ☐

3. a I need to buy a mobile phone. Mine's not working.
   b Some people believe that the mobile phones are bad for your health.
   a ☐   b ☐   both a and b ☐

4. a Nile is the longest river in the world.
   b The Pacific is the largest ocean on Earth.
   a ☐   b ☐   both a and b ☐

5. a I saw a fabulous vase in the market so I haggled with the stall holder to get a better price.
   b The best place to get a bargain is January sales.
   a ☐   b ☐   both a and b ☐

6. a My sister works in the hospital because she's a surgeon.
   b I have to go into hospital for an operation on my knee.
   a ☐   b ☐   both a and b ☐

6 Choose the correct options to complete the email. (Ø = no article).

Hi Elka

How's ⁽¹⁾*the / Ø* life in Germany? I haven't seen you since we left ⁽²⁾*a / Ø* university! That's six months now! Anyway, since then I've been working as ⁽³⁾*a / the* waitress in a restaurant. It's ⁽⁴⁾*a / Ø* good job but I'm a bit bored and I want to do something more challenging. Anyway, yesterday I saw ⁽⁵⁾*an / the* advertisement in the newspaper saying that there were jobs in Germany. ⁽⁶⁾*An / The* ad said that anyone who spoke English could apply. It's with a company that is in ⁽⁷⁾*the / Ø* Black Forest. That's really near your home town, isn't it? If they ask me to come for ⁽⁸⁾*an / Ø* interview, can I stay at your house? If you don't have ⁽⁹⁾*a / the* spare room, I can always sleep on ⁽¹⁰⁾*the / Ø* sofa. That's no problem for me. Would that be OK?

Hope to hear from you soon!

Isobel

BRING IT TOGETHER

7 Complete the text with one word in each gap (*isn't*, etc. = one word).

My world

Nguyen Van Son

Floating markets

Floating markets are a common sight in my country, Vietnam, especially along ⁽¹⁾_____ Mekong River. ⁽²⁾_____ busiest of all of them is the market at Phung Hiep, where you can see hundreds of boats fighting for trade. You can ⁽³⁾_____ eat hot food, cooked on the boat or you can buy fresh ingredients to cook at home. My grandmother worked at the market for years as ⁽⁴⁾_____ cook and I still think of her hot soup whenever I go there.

An important thing about the market is its timetable. Neither the fruit traders ⁽⁵⁾_____ the fisherman work after 11 a.m. so you have to get there early. Many tourists here take ⁽⁶⁾_____ tour around the market and I recommend that too. If you don't speak Vietnamese, you'll ⁽⁷⁾_____ be able to speak to people nor get the best prices for things. Bargaining is ⁽⁸⁾_____ big part of market life, so grab a local guide and let them get all the deals for you!

Skills development

Functional language
Arranging a service

1 Complete the words in the conversations.

1
- **A** We'd like to rent some mountain bikes tomorrow. Can you tell me your daily (1)r _ t _ ?
- **B** The normal bikes are €10 a day, and the mountain bikes are €25.
- **A** OK, and what's your minimum rental (2)p _ r _ _ _ d?
- **B** There isn't one. You can rent them for as long as you like.
- **A** Great! Will I need to pay a (3)d _ p _ _ _ _ t too?
- **B** Yes, it's €60 per person per bike.
- **A** No problem. And one more question. What (4)d _ c _ m _ _ _ _ s do I need?
- **B** We'll need to see your passport or an identity card. OK?
- **A** Yes, that's fine. Thanks very much for your help.

2
- **C** I'd like to get a (1)q _ _ t _ for replacing the carpet in my bedroom. It's really old.
- **D** Certainly. Do you have a (2)b _ d _ _ _ t for the job?
- **C** Yes, I do. I can't really pay more than about $200.
- **D** Well I think we can do that.
- **C** Is there a (3)d _ _ c _ _ _ _ nt if I pay cash?
- **D** No, I'm afraid there isn't. Now, you need to choose the carpet first. I'll show you some samples.
- **C** Oh I don't have a car. Can I arrange for the carpet to be (4)d _ l _ v _ _ _ _ d?
- **D** Yes, yes, don't worry about that. We'll handle everything.
- **C** Great. OK, let's look at the samples then.

Listening
Listening for stress

1 a Look at this introduction to a interview on shopping rip-offs. Underline the words which you think will be stressed the most.

> When you're shopping on the high street do you fork out a lot more money than you expected? Do you know which products are the biggest rip off? Today we speak to retail specialist **Huang Wen** who'll tell you how to save money at the shops.

b 🔊 10.2 Listen and check.

2 🔊 10.3 Listen to the rest of the interview and correct the wrong information.

1. The prices of parking change a lot during the day and there are special deals too.
2. It's best to go online to find the cheapest train tickets.
3. If you want to get something in the sales, you have to go early in the morning.
4. Here's a tip – sales often begin on a Monday when most people are at work.
5. You've been shopping all day for a new leather jacket. You've neither found the right colour nor the right design.
6. How much do you pay for a hot chocolate? £3?
7. Well that's true but with a 100% profit, the café soon pays for all of that!

> **Strategy** In English, the most important words in a sentence always receive more stress than other words in the sentence. When you listen, try to pick out these key words and use them to help you understand the whole conversation.

Skills 10

Writing a CV

Bernice Omanuwa
15 Pickle Street
Durham
DH18 1PW
Home tel. (0191) 4980904
Mob. (07700) 900211
Email bernice@berniceomanuwa.com
1 _____ Nigerian
2 _____ 1 March 1986
3 _____

2012– **Import Manager, Kamble Imports**
Manager for imports of wooden furniture to the UK and Europe. Responsible for liaising with suppliers in China, Nigeria and South Africa. Several successes in achieving new contracts in Wales and Ireland.

2010–2011 **Sales Manager, Worley Candles**
Sales Manager for Worley Candles, which involved dealing with shops throughout the UK. Also developed new range of colourful candles for shop front displays. Managed a team of seven people.

2009–2010 **Sales Assistant, Worley Candles**
Handled orders for the Perceive Candle Range from Nigeria to suppliers in North-West England and Scotland.

4 _____

2004–2008 **BA Hons in Marketing**
Durham Business School, Durham University

2001–2004 **Castlemount School, London**
A level Maths (A), English (A), Economics (A), Chinese (C)
11 GCSEs (Grade A).

5 _____
Dance — Member of local salsa club in Durham. I take part in regular performances with my dance group.
Travel — My dream is to travel to every country in the world.

6 _____
Full clean driving licence.
Fluent in English and Hausa.
Intermediate level Chinese.
Basic programming (Java, C++).

1 Complete gaps 1–6 in the CV with headings from the box.

> Date of birth   Education
> Hobbies and interests   Nationality
> Other skills   Work experience

2 Read the CV again and answer the questions.
1. What did Bernice study at university?
2. How many languages does she speak?
3. What computer skills does she have?
4. What does she do in her spare time?
5. How long has she worked at her current company?
6. How many people's work did she organise in her previous job?
7. What was her weakest school subject when she was 18?
8. What's her post code?

3 a What information would you include in your CV? Make notes about
- personal information
- work experience
- education
- hobbies and interests
- other skills

b Write your CV. Be careful to organise your work clearly.

> **Strategy** When you write a CV, it's important to organise your ideas carefully. Your CV needs to be clear and easy to read, so that it makes a good impression. Make sure you include key information about your skills and experience, but don't write too much – aim for one A4 page.

11 Technology

Vocabulary
Talking about ideas & inventions

1 Read the text and complete the words.

Currently working on...
a flying carpet!

Flying carpets may become a reality, according to Professor Lakshminarayanan Mahadevan of Harvard University. His (1) br _ _ _ _ w _ v _ came from observing the movements of fish-like rays, which swim close to the ocean floor. Mahadevan's (2) b _ _ _ kt _ _ _ _ gh was to apply this observation to movement in the air. He believes it would be possible to make a 'flying' sheet large enough to carry a person, but it would have one major (3) d _ _ wb _ _ k: it wouldn't be very comfortable to ride on! Of course there might be some (4) e _ _ ly a _ _ p _ ers who would be willing to try it, but many feel that the 'flying carpet' idea is just a (5) _ imm _ _ k. However, this technology could still become a (6) co _ _ _ er c _ al su _ _ ess. Some people have suggested that flexible, 'flying' sheets could be used in machines and other useful (7) g _ d _ _ ts.

2 Complete the sentences with the adjective formed from the noun in brackets. Add *-al* and/or *un-* if necessary.

1 I remember watching a programme about astronomy that was really _____ . It made me want to learn all I could about the universe. (inspiration)
2 The _____ idea came from a researcher in France, and was then developed by a team in the US. (origin)
3 New technology has meant that many _____ ways of working have disappeared. (tradition)
4 I think it's _____ to communicate just by writing on social networks. Human beings are meant to speak to each other. (nature)
5 There is a new type of soft, flexible robot which is very different from the _____ , metallic one. (convention)
6 The keys on most keyboards are in an _____ order. It doesn't make any sense! (logic)

3 Complete the conversation with the correct form of the verbs from the box.

| come   figure   get   strike |

A Do you like my T-shirt? I printed it myself.
B Really? It's so unusual! How did you (1)_____ up with the design?
A I saw some similar designs on a website and it (2)_____ me that I could create my own.
B Was it difficult?
A No, not really, although it took a while to (3)_____ out which colours to use!
B How did you print the design onto the fabric?
A I (4)_____ the idea for that from a craft website. I used a special kind of paper and an iron!
B You should start a business making them!

Describing gadgets

4 a Put the letters in brackets in the correct order to make words.

The TouchTunes Virtuo is a jukebox for the twenty-first century. OK, it doesn't have the same shiny (1)_____ (latmelic) case of the 1950s' original or the (2)_____ (nudored) glass cover that keeps the records inside. In fact, this music player is more similar to portable, (3)_____ (lehdnadh) gadgets like MP3 players or smartphones. This (4)_____ (gihh-htce) product allows users to access huge digital music libraries, and to search for songs by genre or lyrics. There are no buttons to press – the screen is (5)_____ (cuhto-tinsvseei) and designed to be operated by someone's finger. It's also incredibly (6)_____ (lmsi), so it hangs on the wall like a picture. The music isn't small though – the sound quality is incredible!

b Look at the photos. Can you think of any other adjectives to describe the gadgets?

VOCABULARY EXTENSION
Computing words

5 a Read the definitions. Complete the sentences with the words and phrases in bold.

> **back up** a copy of your files that you make in case your computer doesn't work
>
> **boot up** to start a computer and get it ready to work
>
> **bug** a mistake in a computer program that stops it working properly
>
> **crash** to stop working suddenly (of a computer)
>
> **hard copy** a paper copy of a file that is on your computer or online
>
> **jargon** technical language used by experts which is not easily understood by other people
>
> **shut down** to turn off your computer when you finish using it
>
> **user-friendly** easy to use by people, straightforward

1. It's very important for gadgets to be _____ as people want to be able to use them quickly and easily.
2. I wish someone would explain what all this _____ means so that I can choose the computer that I need.
3. You should always make a _____ of your files in case your laptop gets stolen.
4. I'll find the website for you in a moment. I just need to _____ the computer.
5. My computer doesn't often _____. It's usually very reliable.
6. We've got some new software at work, which is causing us a lot of problems. Every week we find a new _____ in it.
7. I forgot to _____ my computer before I went to bed, so it was on all night.
8. Could you send me a _____ of that document, please? My printer's not working at the moment.

b 🔊 11.1 Listen and check.

6 Complete the email with the correct forms of the words and phrases in **5a**.

Hi Alberto,
Help! Something's wrong with my computer. Yesterday, I was surfing the internet when my laptop suddenly (1)_____. The picture stopped moving and it wouldn't even (2)_____: I had to take the battery out to stop it! Now, whenever I start the computer, it won't (3)_____. In the beginning, I thought it was a virus, but a colleague of mine told me it was probably a (4)_____ in the program. She printed off some instructions from the internet for me and gave me the (5)_____. But the instructions aren't (6)_____ at all! They're all written in specialist (7)_____ and I don't understand them. Could you come round tomorrow and look at my laptop for me? All my files are on it and if I can't use it, I'll lose months of work because, stupidly, I never made a (8)_____.
Please help!
Morgan

BRING IT TOGETHER

7 Choose the correct options to complete the article.

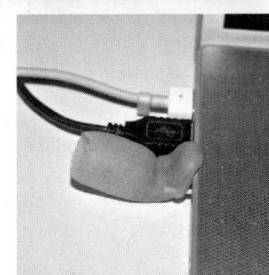

The easiest way to make a (1) *back-up / hard copy* of the files on your computer is to save them on a separate device, like a flash drive. However, there is one big (2) *brainwave / drawback* with these small, portable drives – they're very easy to lose. This isn't a problem for Finnish computer programmer Jerry Jalava, though – his flash drive is one of his fingers! When Jerry lost his finger in a motorbike accident, his doctors joked that he should have a 'finger drive'. Jalava then (3) *struck / figured* out a way of making an artificial finger with a USB drive attached. It's not a (4) *gimmick / bug* – he uses the flash drive to store photos, movies and other files. He even has plans to make another, more (5) *high-tech / high-technology* drive with Wi-Fi and more storage. This 'handheld' device is certainly (6) *unconventional / traditional*!

11

GRAMMAR
Relative clauses

1 a Choose the correct option to complete the sentences. Sometimes both options are correct.

1 Let me show you the present *that / who* I've bought for Xavier.
2 I need to find someone *who / which* speaks Chinese.
3 That's the architect *whose / which* design won an innovation award.
4 Is he the programmer *that / who* started the software company?
5 The place *that / who* does the best coffee is the little café on the corner.
6 This website has lots of unusual gadgets *who / which* might appeal to you.
7 I think the phone number *that / which* I gave you is wrong.
8 A gadget *that / which* has really changed my life is my smartphone.

b In which sentences, 1–8, can we omit the relative pronoun? _____

2 Complete the text with one word in each gap.

3 Add commas to sentences 1–8, if necessary.

1 I need to find a shop where I can buy spare parts for my camera.
2 There is only one drawback to this tablet which is that the battery doesn't last very long.
3 My dad who works for a big IT company always helps me solve my computer problems.
4 We need a faster broadband speed that will let us watch streamed video more easily.
5 Apple which was started by Steve Jobs and Steve Wozniak is now the most profitable computer company in the world.
6 I need to speak to someone who can explain this IT jargon to me.
7 Bill Gates whose Microsoft products are sold all over the world gives huge sums of money to global health and education programmes.
8 Large numbers of people now have mobile phones which has led publishers to create mobile games that are fun to play.

In early 2011, Japanese music fans were all talking about Aimi Eguchi, (1)_____ had just joined the pop group AKB48. She was the girl (2)_____ voice was more beautiful than the other girls'. Almost immediately, she began to play a big role in the band's TV show, (3)_____ amazed fans across the country. After a while, bloggers started to realise why Aimi was so perfect: she didn't really exist!

Aimi was actually a computer-generated character (4)_____ had been created from all the other band members. Bloggers began posting photos of Aimi's face to show the features (5)_____ had been copied from other girls in the band. Her songs, (6)_____ had been recorded by an actor, were digitally adjusted. All the information about her life (7)_____ was on the band's website had been invented too. She wasn't born in 1995 in Saitama, but rather on the keyboards of a team of clever designers. Fans of hers were shocked by the revelation, (8)_____ is hardly surprising. It now remains to be seen whether Aimi will be the beginning of a trend of pixellated pop stars.

So/such

4 Complete the conversation with *so* or *such*.

TREVOR	Good morning, Trevor Jones speaking.
MUM	Hello, Trevor.
TREVOR	Oh, hi Mum. How are you?
MUM	I'm all right. How are you? It's ⁽¹⁾_____ a long time since I last heard from you.
TREVOR	I'm fine, thanks. Mum, you know I'm at work, don't you?
MUM	Yes, yes. I just wanted to check that you got my email yesterday.
TREVOR	I did, yes. I haven't had time to reply yet. Sorry. I've been really busy. I've got ⁽²⁾_____ much work to do.
MUM	Have you? Your sister has too. You're both working ⁽³⁾_____ hard at the moment. Nicole couldn't come home last weekend because she had to work. It was ⁽⁴⁾_____ a shame because we went to see your Auntie Ellen in her new house.
TREVOR	Yes, in your email you said you were sending me some pictures of the house, but there weren't any with the message.
MUM	Oh! I know how that happened! I was in ⁽⁵⁾_____ a rush that I forgot to send them. I'll send them to you now. I took ⁽⁶⁾_____ many photos! Her house is ⁽⁷⁾_____ beautiful. We had ⁽⁸⁾_____ a lovely afternoon there, sitting in her garden.
TREVOR	That's great. Look Mum, I'd better go now. I'll phone you later, OK?
MUM	Oh, yes, of course, dear. Bye!

5 Put *enough* in the correct place to complete the sentences.

1 The computer isn't powerful for the game that I bought.
2 There isn't space here for a music system.
3 I bought a new PC because my old one didn't have a big memory.
4 Do we have food for all the visitors to the IT conference?
5 Matt is talented to run his own software company.

Bring it together

6 a Complete the blog post with the words from the box. There is one word that you don't need.

> enough   so   such (x2)
> which (x3)   who   whose

Space debris

Space is ⁽¹⁾_____ empty that you could travel for light years, and see nothing. That's the theory. Unfortunately, it's no longer true. Since 1957, when the Russians sent the first satellite, Sputnik, into space, thousands of other objects have been left in orbit. Many of these are large ⁽²⁾_____ to do serious damage if they hit other objects. This is a real possibility: in 2011 the International Space Station, ⁽³⁾_____ crew carries out important research, was almost hit by some debris and the crew nearly had to return to Earth. Space debris has become ⁽⁴⁾_____ a big problem that a number of companies are trying to find ways of removing it. One ⁽⁵⁾_____ company is Star Inc. The spacecraft ⁽⁶⁾_____ they are developing is called the EDDE (Electro Dynamic Debris Eliminator) Vehicle. This is a spacecraft ⁽⁷⁾_____ can capture space debris with lightweight nets. However, a machine ⁽⁸⁾_____ can pick up rubbish in space, can also pick up other things, including other countries' satellites. Star Inc. therefore wants EDDE to be controlled by the United Nations so that all the world's governments will support their plan to make space a greener place for everyone!

> **debris** /debri:/ (noun) large pieces of stone, metal, wood etc. that have been left in an area after an accident or a disaster (e.g. an earthquake)

b Which relative pronoun in the text can be omitted?

Skills development

Functional language
Dealing with technical problems

1 Complete the conversation with the correct form of the words from the box.

| already | manage | mean | say | suppose | try |

A Jackie, you're the computer guru. Can you help me with something?

B Yeah! What's the problem?

A I want to put a music program on my tablet. I downloaded it this morning, but it doesn't work. I've finally ⁽¹⁾ _____ to get it started, but I can't get any sound.

B That's strange. What's the program ⁽²⁾ _____ to do?

A To replicate the sounds of musical instruments. It ⁽³⁾ _____ on the box that it's compatible with this tablet.

B What about reinstalling it?

A I've ⁽⁴⁾ _____ tried that, but it didn't work.

B Have you ⁽⁵⁾ _____ looking on the internet? Maybe other people have had the same problem. Let's have a look. They say here that you're ⁽⁶⁾ _____ to download some software before using the program.

A Really? And then it'll work?

B I think so. Let's give it a go, shall we?

Listening
Listening to longer conversations

1 a 🔊 11.2 Look at the photo and make notes about the questions.
  1 Where are the people?
  2 What job do you think they do?
  3 What kind of questions do you think they have to answer?

  b Listen and check your ideas.

2 Listen again and choose the correct answer a, b or c.

1 Where was Nikhil when he was given the leaflet for the job?
  a outside the university library
  b outside a computer shop
  c outside the call centre

2 What does Nikhil say about his wages at the call centre?
  a They were very high.
  b They were very low.
  c They were average.

3 What was not shown on the computer on the wall of the call centre?
  a the length of each call
  b the number of people waiting
  c the name and address of the caller

4 Which of these people did Nikhil not like in this job?
  a his boss
  b the customers
  c his colleagues

5 What was wrong with one customer's handheld games player?
  a It was completely broken.
  b There was a cable missing.
  c The battery hadn't been charged.

6 Why couldn't one customer install the program she wanted?
  a There was something wrong with the disk.
  b She didn't have the disk.
  c She'd put the disk into the wrong place.

7 Why didn't one man's computer boot up?
  a He hadn't turned it on.
  b It had a virus.
  c There was a problem with the screen.

8 Where does Nikhil work now?
  a in a design company
  b in another call centre
  c in a software company

> **Strategy** When you listen to a long conversation, you won't always understand everything, but don't panic!
> - Listen for key information to answer the questions.
> - Think about the context of the audio. Does this give you any clues about what the speakers are saying?
> - Don't stop listening if you hear a word that you don't understand.

SKILLS 11

READING Using pictures

1 a Look at images 1–4 and choose the best sentence to describe the machine.

   a The Thing-O-Matic is used to make 3D images of plastic objects so that you can keep the images on your computer.
   b The Thing-O-Matic is used to make plastic objects at home, with the help of your computer.
   c The Thing-O-Matic is used to clean objects using special chemicals.

b Read the text and check your answers.

2 Complete the gaps in the text with sentences a–g. There is one sentence that you do not need.

   a That takes most people about 12 hours, apparently.
   b It can even make spare parts for itself!
   c This USB cable transfers the data to the machine, just like a normal printer.
   d It was a disaster with no solution in sight.
   e White layers began to appear on a sort of moving platform.
   f The project is in development right now, but it could be on the market within five years.
   g He's the sort of man who takes a whole week to put an Ikea chest of drawers together.

I think I'll just make a thingamajig…

My four-year-old daughter was sitting on the floor crying. We were at my friend Ali's house and his dog had just bitten the head off her favourite toy, a plastic dinousaur. (1)_____ That was until Ali told us to follow him with the cryptic comment, 'Don't worry about your T-Rex. I'll make you a new one!'

Feeling slightly suspicious, we all followed him to the garage where he showed us a wooden box that was connected to his computer. When Ali told me he had built this device from a kit, I could hardly believe my eyes. (2)_____ Now he was telling us that he had made this machine: the Thing-O-Matic.

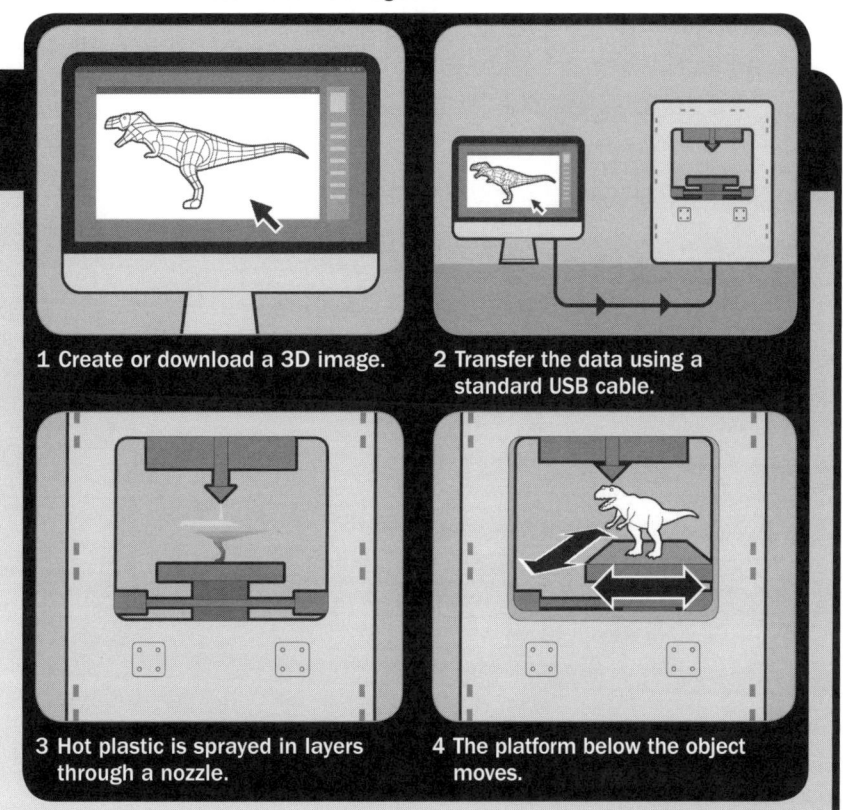

Ali put the dinosaur on a special device and created a 3D image of it on his computer. Once this was done, he sent the image to this mysterious box, which began to whirr and vibrate. Then hot plastic shot out of a special nozzle. (3)_____ Before our eyes, an exact replica of the dinosaur began to appear. To my daughter, it was nothing short of magic (and to be honest, it felt the same to me too).

The amazing thing is that the Thing-O-Matic is available for anyone who wants one. It comes by mail order at €1,299, which includes all the software you need. The only drawback is that you have to assemble it yourself. (4)_____ But if Ali can do it, anyone can.

The machine was the brainwave of MakerBot Industries in New York City. It can produce toys, tools, or almost anything in plastic. (5)_____

The really exciting thing about the Thing-O-Matic is that this is just the beginning. At the moment, the main innovation is that it can model things in plastic, but it could soon work with metals and other materials too. There is even the possibility that a similar device could make an entire mobile phone. And there's not long to wait until you can buy one! (6)_____ Tell me that isn't magic! My daughter certainly thinks so!

1 Create or download a 3D image.
2 Transfer the data using a standard USB cable.
3 Hot plastic is sprayed in layers through a nozzle.
4 The platform below the object moves.

STRATEGY Reading texts often include pictures or photos. Study these images carefully before you read to help you understand any new vocabulary or complicated descriptions.

12 OUT OF THE ORDINARY

VOCABULARY
Experiences

1 Circle the word that <u>doesn't</u> work in each conversation.

1. **A** What was the best moment of your trip to Costa Rica?
   B I remember one morning when we were camping and I woke up very early. It was *dawn / sunrise / twilight*, and the rainforest was absolutely beautiful.

2. **A** Do you remember our trip to Iceland?
   B Oh yeah – walking along the rocks by the sea *in the dead of night / at dusk / at twilight*, just as it was getting dark. Magic!

3. **A** You look exhausted, Miriam! What's wrong?
   B I didn't get much sleep last night. I had to get up at *daybreak / at sunset / in the dead of night* to drive my brother to the airport. He had a 6 a.m. flight!

4. **A** What's your favourite time of day?
   B Well, I love *dusk / late afternoon / mid-morning*. At weekends I love sitting in the garden in the bright sunshine and just having a rest.

5. **A** What do you like to do when you finish work in the evening?
   B I like to walk home by the river where I can look at the mountains *at dawn / at sunset / in the twilight*.

6. **A** What time shall I call you tomorrow?
   B Well, I'm busy from 8.00 to 10.00 a.m. and then again from 2.00 to 4.30 p.m., so *early morning / late afternoon / mid-morning* would be best.

2 Complete the adjectives and intensifiers in the email.

> To Beppe,
> Hello from Arizona! We visited the Grand Canyon yesterday – it was (1) a _ e _ _ _ _ e! We drove there and the whole journey was (2) a _ s _ l _ t _ _ _ y (3) b _ _ _ th-t _ k _ _ _ g. We had to go along mountain roads with no walls to protect us if there was an accident! But it was worth it because the Canyon is really (4) _ w _ -in _ _ ir _ _ g. The views are truly spectacular. The best moment was at dusk – watching the sun go down over the rocks was a (5) t _ t _ _ _ _ _ (6) o _ _ rw _ _ _ _ _ _ g experience. I've got some (7) st _ _ n _ _ _ g photos to show you when we get back!
> Love,
> Lucy

3 a Match 1–4 to a–d to make four expressions.

1. Riding in a helicopter over São Paolo at dusk. That memory really sticks ___
2. When I saw my beautiful wife on our wedding day. She really took ___
3. Going to my first football match at the stadium. When I saw the crowd, I couldn't believe ___
4. When I was invited to watch a movie being filmed. It was a once ___

a. out for me.
b. my eyes!
c. in a lifetime experience.
d. my breath away.

b What question do you think the people in **3a** are answering?

Night expressions

4 Complete the text with the words from the box. There is one word that you don't need.

| call | crack | get | long | nights | overnight | shifts | sleep | stay |

Hidden dangers

In my job I often have to do night (1)_____ . This means working all night (2)_____ , five nights a week. It pays well, but I've read that working (3)_____ can be bad for your health. Apparently, you're more likely to suffer from obesity, diabetes and heart disease.
The article explained that these risks don't affect people who occasionally (4)_____ up all night at a party or go on an (5)_____ bus journey. The problem is if your routine changes a lot – if you go to bed at 11 p.m. one night and then at the (6)_____ of dawn the next. This can sometimes happen to people who do a lot of on (7)_____ work, as they often have to (8)_____ some sleep during the day. This can be bad for their sleep pattern and sometimes, their general health.

Idiomatic expressions

5 Choose the correct options to complete the conversations.

1. A Dan told me you saw a bear when you were on holiday in Sweden.
   B Yeah, it was amazing. It really stopped us in our *shoes / tracks*!
2. A I love having a cat. It sounds silly, but she's really good company.
   B Well I suppose friends come in all *forms / shapes* and sizes!
3. A Shall we go to the beach tomorrow?
   B Yes, good idea. We should *make / put* the most of the good weather.
4. A We're going to Toulouse for our next holiday.
   B Really? *Do / Take* the time to visit Albi too. There's a great museum there.
5. A Has having children changed your life, Marija?
   B Absolutely. Now I have the girls, I *see / look* things in a different light.
6. A I had a real 'aha' moment at work today. I felt really pleased!
   B Yeah, it's really satisfying when the penny *drops / falls* like that.

VOCABULARY EXTENSION
Further idiomatic expressions

6 Match the idiomatic expressions in bold in 1–6 to definitions a–f.

1. I got an email from an old classmate today completely **out of the blue**. I hadn't spoken to him for years! ____
2. Don't buy souvenirs at the airport. They **cost an arm and a leg** there. ____
3. We're not sure if we're going on holiday. Everything's **up in the air** at the moment. ____
4. We only caught the train **by the skin of our teeth**. The doors were closing, but we managed to jump on! ____
5. Thinking of my favourite memory is **easier said than done**. There are too many to choose from! ____
6. I was planning a surprise birthday party for Rita, but she found out. Charlie **let the cat out of the bag** by accident! ____

a tell somebody something that was secret (by mistake)
b be very expensive
c from nowhere, without expecting it, without warning
d something that sounds easy, but is actually difficult to do
e with very little time remaining
f unconfirmed, not yet decided

7 a Complete the sentences with expressions from **6**.

1. A I'm really disappointed with these photos – they don't look good at all.
   B Well, taking good pictures at sunset is _____ .
2. Lana hadn't told anyone that she was pregnant, but I _____ by mistake. I sent her a message on Facebook to say congratulations!
3. A Did you have a good time in China?
   B Fantastic! The best bit was sailing on the Yangtze River, although we only caught the boat _____ .
4. We've got tickets to the Champions League final, but they _____ . We can't afford to go out for the rest of the month!
5. A Is it true that you're going to Bhutan next summer?
   B I hope so, but's all _____ at the moment. I need to find out whether I can get a visa.
6. My boss has given me a promotion! I wasn't expecting it at all – it was totally _____ .

b 🔊 12.1 Listen and check your answers.

BRING IT TOGETHER

8 Correct the underlined mistakes in the text.

Night life in Puerto Rico

At (1)<u>dust</u>, we got into our canoes and followed our guide out into the lagoon. Paddling the canoes was (2)<u>easy</u> said than done as the water was quite rough, but ahead of us we could see an (3)<u>awe-inspired</u> view of the hills above Vieques. They soon disappeared into darkness.

It was the (4)<u>death</u> of night when we finally stopped paddling. Everything was dark and there was no moon in the sky. Then it began.

At first, it was just a flash of light in the water. Soon, the whole lagoon was a cloud of bright blue. We couldn't (5)<u>belief</u> our eyes as the water shone with an amazing light, generated by tiny creatures under the water. I just kept looking and looking at it. I wanted to (6)<u>take</u> the most of it because it was so beautiful. We got back to the beach at the (7)<u>start</u> of dawn, exhausted and amazed. It was a (8)<u>one</u> in a lifetime experience, and the best moment of my trip to the Caribbean.

A great piece of work, Ahmed! There are just a few mistakes – please can you correct them?

1 _____   2 _____   3 _____
4 _____   5 _____   6 _____
7 _____   8 _____

12

Grammar
Reporting verbs

1 Choose the correct options to complete the conversations.

1. A What happened when you spoke to Martin?
   B He agreed *helping / to help* me arrange the expedition.
2. A Why are we leaving at dawn?
   B The guide advised us *setting off / to set off* early because it gets very hot in the afternoon.
3. A We were waiting for your phone call all afternoon!
   B I do apologise for *not calling / not to call* you.
4. A Who was that man?
   B He claimed *being / to be* a tour guide, but I didn't believe him.
5. A What happened when the police spoke to those pickpockets?
   B They denied *doing / to do* anything and the police just let them go!
6. A Why were you angry with the car rental company?
   B Because they blamed me *for damaging / to damage* the car!

2 Look at the text messages. Rewrite the sentences in bold using the words in brackets. Keep the same meaning.

1 I'm sorry I forgot to call you earlier! Speak tonight? xx
I apologise for forgetting to call you earlier! (apologise)

2 The meeting went really well – my boss told me I gave a great presentation!
_____ (congratulated)

3 Do you want to come sailing this weekend? **Dad promised that he'd take us!**
_____ (agreed)

4 **Denise and Sam would like us to have dinner with them.** Are you free on Thursday? X
_____ (invited)

5 **Nikos said we should go to the cinema tonight.** What do you think? Carl
_____ (suggested)

6 Just went to buy a newspaper... **The shop assistant thought I'd stolen it!!**
_____ (accused)

3 Complete the text using the correct form of the words in brackets.

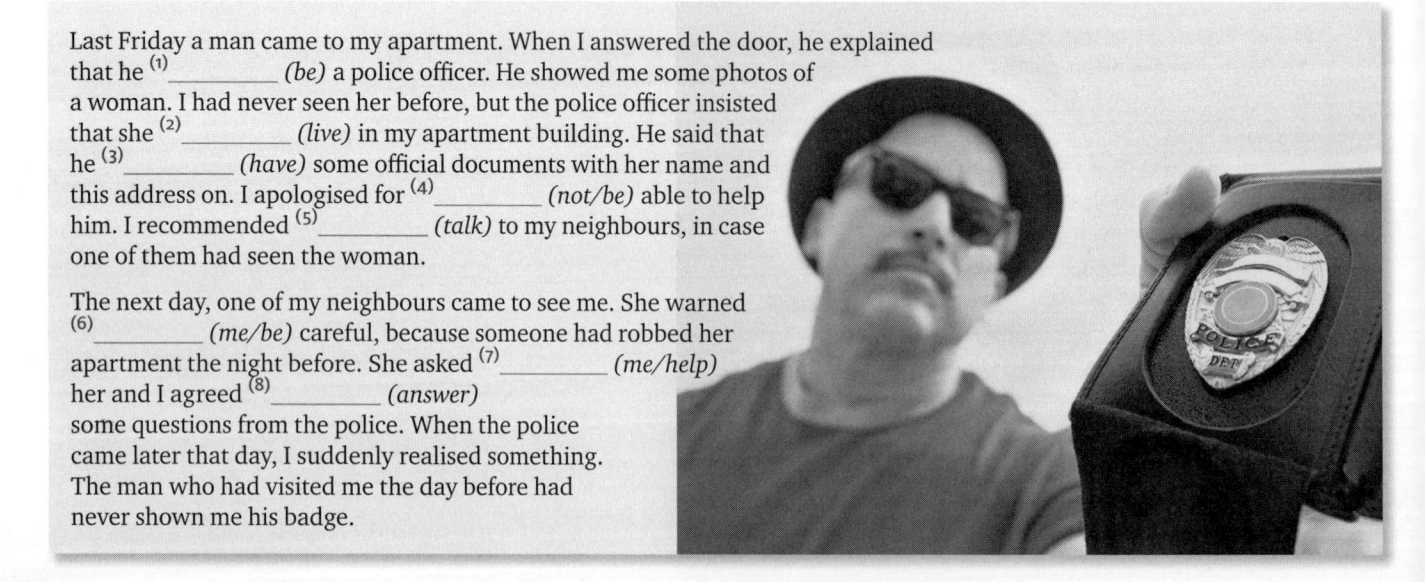

Last Friday a man came to my apartment. When I answered the door, he explained that he ⁽¹⁾_____ (be) a police officer. He showed me some photos of a woman. I had never seen her before, but the police officer insisted that she ⁽²⁾_____ (live) in my apartment building. He said that he ⁽³⁾_____ (have) some official documents with her name and this address on. I apologised for ⁽⁴⁾_____ (not/be) able to help him. I recommended ⁽⁵⁾_____ (talk) to my neighbours, in case one of them had seen the woman.

The next day, one of my neighbours came to see me. She warned ⁽⁶⁾_____ (me/be) careful, because someone had robbed her apartment the night before. She asked ⁽⁷⁾_____ (me/help) her and I agreed ⁽⁸⁾_____ (answer) some questions from the police. When the police came later that day, I suddenly realised something. The man who had visited me the day before had never shown me his badge.

Review: perfect & continuous

4 Choose the correct options to complete the sentences.

1 Aaron *is working / has been working* nights since March.
2 Sara fell off her bike when she *had come / was coming* home yesterday.
3 I can't see you on Thursday evening because *I'll have worked / I'll be working* then.
4 I woke up at the crack of dawn because *I'd set / I've set* my alarm for the wrong time!
5 *I've tried / I'm trying* to get fit at the moment so that I can go hiking later in the year.
6 Let's go out. *We've been sitting / We're sitting* indoors all day.
7 By seven o'clock last night I felt exhausted because *I've driven / I'd been driving* since dawn.
8 *We'll have done / We'll be doing* all of our assignments by the end of January.

5 Complete the web chat with an appropriate form of the verb in brackets. Use perfect or continuous verb forms.

MarliesW says: Hi Vic, how's it going? Excited about your holiday?

Victoria321 says: Definitely! I (1)_____ (really/look) forward to it. I (2)_____ (work) night shifts for the past few weeks so I'm exhausted.

MarliesW says: Yeah, you really deserve a few days off! ☺ Have you found somewhere to stay?

Victoria321 says: Well, we (3)_____ (not/book) anything... until last night! We (4)_____ (think) that we would just find a campsite when we arrived. But I (5)_____ (look) online last night when I found a lovely campsite near the beach, so we decided to stay there. It looks really peaceful – by the time we've spent a few days there, we (6)_____ (forget) all about work!

MarliesW says: Sounds great! Well, we should meet for a drink sometime this week – it would be nice to see you before you go. What about Thursday evening?

Victoria321 says: Sorry, can't do Thursday – I (7)_____ (work) then.

MarliesW says: Oh yeah, sorry! ☹ Why don't we meet on Friday afternoon, then? Go for a coffee.

Victoria321 says: OK. Let's try the new Italian cafe on George Street – I (8)_____ (want) to go there for ages.

MarliesW says: Perfect! See you there at 4.30?

Victoria321 says: Sounds good. ☺ Sorry M, I have got to go... Shift starts in 45 mins! See you Friday! x x x

Victoria321 is offline.

BRING IT TOGETHER

6 Complete the blog post with one word in each gap (*isn't*, etc. = one word).

Mum's Blog World – Yuki Kamimura

Simple pleasures

Before I became a parent, everyone warned me (1)_____ it's really hard work. Even when they were congratulating me (2)_____ becoming a mother, people were saying how difficult my life would be. They told me, 'In a few months you won't remember what it feels like to sleep all night long. You'll (3)_____ dreaming of a having a lie-in, being able to wake up when you want!' It's true: looking after a baby is exhausting, but it's also great fun! My daughter Satako is two and half now. Today, we (4)_____ just been laughing all day because her uncle and aunt are here. They arrived yesterday and they can't believe how much (5)_____ grown and what she can do! When they last came, she (6)_____ learned to walk, but now she's running around everywhere.

When people ask me (7)_____ explain how it feels to be a mum, I just tell them that it's all about these simple pleasures: spending time with family and living in the moment. Before I had Satako, I'd (8)_____ working long hours for many years, so now I really enjoy being with her and sharing her excitement about all the new things she's experiencing. It makes you see the world around you in a different light.

Skills development

Functional language Showing interest

1 Complete the words to make a conversation.

A	How was your weekend?
B	Well – not very good! I had to go to hospital on Saturday!
A	Hospital? What (1) h_____ ?
B	Do you really want me to tell you?
A	Yeah, (2) g_____ on then.
B	Well, I was chopping some vegetables and I cut my finger.
A	You're (3) j_____ !
B	I'm not. There was blood everywhere. I had to call an ambulance.

A	You (4) d_____ !
B	What else could I do? There was only me in the house!
A	Ah, poor (5) t_____ !
B	Anyway, I went to hospital...
A	Carry (6) o_____ .
B	Well, that was it. I got to the hospital, blood all over my shirt, and I had six stitches!
A	(7) N_____ way!
B	It's true! Look!
A	Eeuw! No, I don't want to!

Listening Activating background knowledge

1 a What do you know about the event in the photo? Make notes about the questions.

1 What event does the photo show?
   _____

2 Where can you see it?
   _____

3 When can you see it?
   _____

b 🔊 12.2 Listen to two people talking about the event. Check your answers.

Strategy Sometimes you can use your background knowledge to help you understand difficult listening texts. Before you listen, think about what you already know about the topic and ask yourself questions about it.

2 Listen again and complete Anna's notes. Write one word in each gap.

> Stuart went to see the aurora borealis in (1) _____ .
>
> He didn't see it on the first night because it was too (2) _____ .
>
> Stuart said that the lights reminded him of a (3) _____ fiction film.
>
> The aurora borealis is named after the Roman Goddess of (4) _____ .
>
> The lights are usually (5) _____ or green.
>
> The best times of year to see it are (6) _____ or spring.

Strategy When you have to complete sentences, follow the instructions exactly. Don't write too many words! Remember to read your sentences afterwards, to check that they make sense.

Skills 12

Writing Checking your work

Hartnell Hire – Venezuela
★ ★ ★ ★

Young couple – Chloe and Ian

Neither of us has a driving licence, so we decided to hire some bikes to explore the beautiful island of Isla Margarita, off the coast of Venezuela. Luckily, we found Hartnell Hire, a little bike shop that rented bikes to us. It's a fabulous way to explore this island paradise!

The shop itself is easy to find in the main tourist area of Palomar, near Avenida Santiago Mariño. The island is quite mountainous, so we hired mountain bikes, which cost $10 a day. You need to leave a deposit of $50, which they return at the end of your trip. The shop staff will ask to see each cyclist's ID card or passport, but you don't have to leave it with them.

The bikes we hired were in good condition. The company also gave us helmets and gloves, although the helmets' straps were a bit old and they were difficult to adjust.

The shop owner, Carlos, was really friendly and he gave us a lot of information about the island's cycle routes. On Day 1 we went up into the mountains, and on Day 2 we took the more gentle path along the beaches and through the local fishing villages. It was a great experience, although the routes' uphill climbs were so steep that we had to get off the bikes and push them. We should have listened to other people's advice – some of the routes aren't recommended for beginner cyclists, like us!

All in all, we definitely recommend Hartnell Hire. There was only one problem (which is why we haven't given them a top rating). When we returned the bikes, there was nobody in the shop. Its opening hours were supposed to be 5.00–8.00 p.m., but we arrived at 5.00 and had to wait for almost an hour before Carlos' assistant finally arrived.

---

1 Read the review. Number the topics 1–6 in the order that they are mentioned.

  a ☐ the equipment
  b ☐ whether they would recommend the service
  c ☐ what the actual activity was like
  d ☐ what kind of people wrote the review
  e ☐ the shop's requirements
  f ☐ why they decided to do the activity

2 **a** Read the review again. Underline examples of apostrophes (').

  b Complete the chart with examples from the review.

We use an apostrophe to...	Example
show a contraction.	*It's,* (1)_____
show possession. • After a singular noun we add *'s*. • After a singular noun or name that ends in *s*, we can add *'* or *'s*. • After a plural noun ending in *s* we just add *'*. • After a plural noun that doesn't end in *s*, we add *'s*.	(2)_____ (3)_____ (4)_____ (5)_____
Remember! We don't use an apostrophe with *it* to show possession.	*Its opening hours*

3 Think about a time when you used a service, or did an activity, like the one in the review. Make short notes about your experience, using the notes in **1** to help you.

4 **a** Write a review of your experience.

  b Check your work for mistakes. Make sure you have used apostrophes correctly.

> **Strategy** When you write, it's important to use punctuation like apostrophes correctly. Always check your work carefully for mistakes.

PROGRESS TEST 4

GRAMMAR & VOCABULARY
(25 points)

1 Rewrite the sentences using the word in bold. Do not change the word given. *(10 points)*

0 We're visiting the accounts department tomorrow.
   We'll be visiting the accounts department tomorrow. **be**

1 Vincent won't be the architect of the new stadium. Lara also won't be the architect.
   _____ **neither**

2 I was working for hours. Then I decided to have a break.
   _____ **been**

3 Mr Lukas was the Physics teacher. His classes were in the old Science lab.
   _____ **whose**

4 Carol's still cycling. She started at the crack of dawn.
   _____ **since**

5 We had never tried the experiment before. The results were a complete surprise.
   _____ **having**

2 Circle the option that <u>doesn't</u> work. *(7 points)*

0 I think I'll buy this (aluminium) / cotton / nylon shirt.
1 Our software company is sure to be a success. If you invest in it, there'll be *capital / some profit / a return* for you.
2 I'm worried about my business because we have a lot of *debt / grants / loans* to repay to the bank.
3 My sister refuses to use any products made from or produced by animals like *leather / mahogany / silk*.
4 Sophie's *brainwave / drawback / breakthrough* came after she had looked at the results of the experiment.
5 They designed this gadget to be *lightweight / slim / touch-sensitive* to fit in your pocket or a small bag.
6 Bats usually appear in the evening, so the best time to photograph them is at *daybreak / at dusk / in the twilight*.
7 The views of Niagara Falls are *absolutely / completely / very* breath-taking.

3 Complete the sentences with the words from the box. There is one word that you don't need. *(8 points)*

| breath | call | done | figure | fork |
| rubber | ~~run~~ | shapes | tracks | |

0 Can you go to the shops? We've <u>run</u> out of soy sauce.
1 The problem with these budget airlines is that you always have to _____ out extra money to pay for your luggage.
2 We've bought a red _____ bone for the dog to play with. She loves it!
3 I can't _____ out what's wrong with my computer.
4 Getting this project finished on time is easier said than _____ .
5 Our journey down the Amazon was spectacular. It took my _____ away.
6 I've been awake all night so I really need to _____ some sleep.
7 Mobile phones these days come in all _____ and sizes.
8 As soon as we turned the corner, we just stopped in our _____ . There was an awe-inspiring view of the mountains, right in front of us.

READING *(25 points)*

1 Choose the best title for the text. *(3 points)*
  1 Our four-legged friends will show us the future
  2 Nature is the mother of invention
  3 Nasty in nature... but lovely in the lab!

2 Decide if the sentences are true or false. *(12 points)*
  1 Cockroaches can eat products that are made of a kind of paper. _____
  2 The bodies of insects are sometimes more complicated than a human's. _____
  3 Dr Guha has asked the government to officially recognise his invention. _____
  4 Dr Frank Fish was inspired by the tail of the whale. _____
  5 Lotuses die if they are in a very dirty environment. _____
  6 Dr Barthlott copied the smooth leaves of the lotus. _____

3 Complete the sentences with the cockroach, the whale, the lotus or none of them. *(10 points)*
  1 _____ inspired gadgets for entertainment.
  2 An invention based on _____ will help create electricity.
  3 An invention inspired by _____ could be used to decorate your house.
  4 An idea based on _____ was used to improve an existing invention.
  5 _____ has inspired an invention that could save someone's life.

TEST 4

Where might the next big idea in science come from? Surprisingly, it might be hiding behind your cooker or growing quietly in the mid-morning sunshine. That's because more and more scientists have been drawing their inspiration from the world around them. Nature is the new big thing and it's been given a name: 'biomimicry'.

Cockroaches. They're everywhere. They can eat almost anything, even cardboard. Experts believe that they could even survive a nuclear war. We may think they're ugly horrible small black pests, but maybe we should be following the old advice; 'if you can't beat them, join them'. Having realised that cockroaches are super-survivors, Indian scientist Sujoy Guha invented a new artificial heart based on a cockroach's. A human heart has four valves to control the movement of blood, but a cockroach's has 13, so it's a much stronger organ. Guha has already applied for a patent for his invention.

Inspiration can come from the big as well as the small. One day, the aptly named American scientist Dr Frank Fish was walking round an exhibition when he noticed special shapes on a model of a whale. They were on the fins, which are the parts that a whale uses to move. He thought that they had made a mistake because the fins should be smooth. Having spoken to the designers, he learned that the model was accurate. These shapes on the fins help the animal to swim more quickly. Suddenly, he had a brainwave. Copying this design, he created enhanced wind farms, the machines that make energy.

Biomimicry isn't just a question of copying animals. Dr. Wilhelm Barthlott noticed that although lotus flowers grow in very dirty areas, their leaves are always clean. He discovered that they are very rough, and this encourages dirty water to fall off them. After four years of research and development, a German company has now developed a paint which replicates this effect, using his ideas. It never gets dirty!

So it seems like the secret to the future is to imitate nature – but remember, it doesn't always come from the most beautiful plants and animals. New ideas can come from anywhere – even under the kitchen sink!

LISTENING (25 points)

1 🔊 T4 Listen to a radio interview about a trip to Petra in Jordan. Decide if Malikah likes ☺ or doesn't like ☹ these things. Circle the correct answers. (18 points)

0 Petra
1 Jordan in the Indiana Jones films
2 travelling by jeep
3 prices in Jordan
4 the tourists in Petra
5 the weather in Jordan
6 the tour group that she went with
7 riding on camels.
8 the tents in the Bedouin camp
9 talking on the radio

2 Listen again. Answer the questions. (7 points)
0 What time is the radio show broadcast?
   It's broadcast late afternoon.
1 What does Malikah say about the temple in the rock?
2 How long should visitors spend in Petra?
3 Why does Petra suggest getting a guide?
4 What is the best time of day to visit Petra?
5 What does Malikah warn people to do?
6 How did Malikah hear about the Bedouin camp?
7 When did Malikah really enjoy the view of the desert?

WRITING (25 points)

1 Complete the survey with one word in each gap (5 points).

Night work survey – City Paints Ltd

Last week, we sent a questionnaire to all staff. Here (0) _are_ the results of the survey. We found that (1)_____ three-quarters of staff (80%) were happy with the present arrangements. (2)_____ vast majority of people said that the factory was a safe and friendly working environment. All the teams said they were happy with the night shift system, (3)_____ one exception: the delivery department complained that their shift begins at 3 a.m. One of our (4)_____ interesting results was about the staff breakfast. All night workers said that they enjoyed this moment at dawn when everyone takes a break together. People were also happy with the safety arrangements, lighting and heating when the factory is in operation all night long. (5)_____ conclusion, it seems that the factory is well-organised throughout its 24-hour operation, and so we should give credit to the management for their hard work.

2 You have a job at an IT college. The new students have just completed this survey about their computer habits. Write a survey report using the information below. (20 points)

Link Up Computer College – New Students survey

Male: 17 *Female:* 16
US: 7 *China:* 9 *India:* 1 *Mexico:* 2 *UK:* 4 *Canada:* 6 *Switzerland:* 4
Preferred Browser – Internet Explorer: 21
Google Chrome: 11 *Safari:* 1
Operating System – Windows: 32 *Snow Leopard:* 1
Gadgets owned – Laptop 33 *Tablet (iPAD etc):* 15 *eReader (Kindle etc.):* 3 *Blackberry:* 0

Selected Transcripts

1.1, p. 3, Ex 6

1 It was typical! It was about ten years ago and we were going on holiday in the car. We set off really early in the morning, at about, er, 5 a.m. We picked up my cousin at her house and then we started our journey to the beach. It was a really sunny day and everyone was in a really good mood when, suddenly, the car broke down! It just stopped – in the middle of nowhere! It was awful. Dad thought he could sort the problem out but it was too difficult for him. So, we had to call for help. When the mechanic came, he said the car was in a really bad condition and it needed two weeks to repair it. So we just gave up and went home. My mum was really unhappy. I don't think she spoke to my dad for a week!

2 Once, I was working in the university library with my friends. We were under a lot of pressure because we had to hand in a big project later that day. Suddenly, the fire alarm went off. At first, we just ignored it – the university tests the fire alarms at 3pm every Wednesday, so we carried on working as normal. I was just writing down the last part of the report when a security guard came in and shouted at us to leave the building. There really was a fire – at 3 p.m. on Wednesday! Apparently, someone threw a cigarette away while it was still lit and some paper in the bin caught fire.

1.2, p. 6, Exs 1 & 2

1   A: Hello. I'm Nick.
    B: Julieta. Nice to meet you, Nick.
    A: Are you with the bride or the groom, Julieta?
    B: I know the bride, Vera. She's my best friend, in fact!
    A: Right, OK. So, er how did you meet?
    B: We studied Spanish together in Buenos Aires. I have a photo of us actually. Would you like to see it?
    A: Sure.
    B: Look – here we are with our classmates, there were twelve of us altogether. That's me on the left. And Vera is here.
    A: Oh yeah. I see her. It's a great picture.
    B: Thanks. So are you a friend of Dan, the groom?
    A: Yeah, that's right. I'm a friend of the family. I've known Dan since he was a baby.
    B: And now you're here at the wedding! That's so nice. Where are you from then, Nick?
    A: Canada. I just flew in to Boston yesterday.
    B: Really? I think you brought the cold weather with you. It's freezing today! It must be about two degrees out there.
    A: Hmm, well, it was -10 at home in Ottawa when I left!

2   C: Paula! Welcome to Hong Kong! It's so good to see you! How was the flight?
    D: Not bad, thanks. I feel exhausted now though!
    C: Yeah, I bet. Did you manage to sleep on the plane?
    D: Well, a bit, but a funny thing happened. I found my seat on the plane, sat down, and then I glanced over at the row next to me, and I realised that the person sitting there was Michaela, you know, from my old office!
    C: You're joking! Really? You were quite close friends, weren't you? She's the girl with the curly hair, right?
    D: Yeah, that's her. It was such a coincidence! We spent most of the flight talking, catching up on each other's news.
    C: So what is she doing at the moment?
    D: Well, she was studying for a diploma in business but she's dropped out. She didn't enjoy the course because she didn't get on well with her classmates.
    C: Oh, that's a shame. Anyway, let me take your bag. You can tell me the rest of your news in the car.

2.1, p. 12, Ex 1

A: Hello, welcome to Park Lane surgery. How can I help you?
B: Oh, hello. Err, my name's Jennifer Chan. I wonder if you could give me some advice? I'm travelling to India next month – could you tell me if I need any vaccinations?
A: Certainly. One moment, please. Right, it says here that you'll need two different injections.
B: OK. Would it be possible to get the vaccinations in the surgery?
A: Yes, but you'll have to make an appointment with Nurse Green. She's available on Monday, Wednesday and Thursday afternoon.
B: OK... Do you have any idea how long the appointment will take?
A: Uh, you'll need about 20 minutes for the appointment. There are appointments available at 2 p.m. and 4.35 on Thursday. Would either of those be suitable?
B: Yes, I'll come at 4.35. Would you mind writing that on a card for me? I don't have my diary and, um, I'll probably forget otherwise!
A: Of course, here you are. We'll see you on Thursday 12th October at 4.35.
B: Great. Thanks very much for your help.

2.2, p. 12, Ex 1 & 2

A: Today in Ask the Expert, we're with top vet Alexandra Haynes. Our first caller is Gemma Truman from Birmingham. What's your question, Gemma?
B: Hello?
C: Hi, Gemma.
B: Well, I want to become a vet when I leave school. I wonder if you could give me some advice about studying Veterinary Science?
C: OK, well, there are many different kinds of vets. A lot of vets work with small animals – family pets, like hamsters and cats. Other vets work on farms with animals like sheep, horses and so on. I used to work on a dairy farm – I learned a lot about working with large animals. That's very useful in my current job, at a safari park – I work with a lot of exotic animals these days!
B: I think I'd like to work with horses.
C: Fantastic. There are lots of jobs in that area. Uh... How old are you, Gemma?
B: 16.
C: Right, great. Whatever you do, choose the right school subjects next year. If you want to do Veterinary Science at university, you need to study Biology, Chemistry and Maths.
B: Oh, OK... Well, Maths isn't my best subject, but I really like Science. My highest marks are always in Biology!
C: That's good. And I guess you really like animals?
B: Yes, I do. I love horse riding – I ride at a local farm about four times a week. I'm also doing some volunteer work at an animal shelter near my home. We look after dogs without owners.
C: Perfect. Universities want to know that you have hands-on experience of working with animals. Volunteering is an excellent idea.
B: Great!
C: Now, the other thing I should tell you is that veterinary work can be hard. The hours aren't really a problem – they can be long, but you'll quickly get used to that. No, you need to be prepared to see some very badly injured animals. Sometimes, you have to decide if an animal will live or die. It's important to be tough, as well as kind.
B: I think I can do that.
A: Any last words of advice, Alexandra?
C: Mm, yes. It takes five years at university to become a vet – that's a lot of studying! Courses can be very expensive, especially because you'll need to travel around the country to do work experience. If I were you, I'd talk to someone about money before you start university, maybe a family member, or someone from your bank. You don't want to drop out of the course because of the cost!

A: OK, Alexandra, thank you very much. Gemma, has that answered your questions?
B: Yes, definitely. Thank you.
C: My pleasure. Good luck, Gemma!

🔊 3.2, p. 18, Exs 1 & 2

And now for an update on tomorrow's weather. There will be very mixed conditions across the country, including two severe weather warnings. Our first warning is for Cape Town, where there will be dense fog in the early morning. Visibility will be poor for many people in the region, so please drive carefully. Further along the coast, in Port Elizabeth, there will be heavy rain throughout the day. In Durban, however, conditions are much brighter: there will be clear skies and warm weather all day long.

Inland, it's a very different story. Here in Pretoria, temperatures will drop overnight and it will be cold and icy all morning. There's a low of -1°C but it will be warmer in the afternoon, with temperatures reaching 12 degrees in some areas. We could also see some light hail at about 3 or 4 o'clock. In the capital, Johannesburg, it will be a warmer day, but thunder and lightning are likely during the early afternoon. Lastly, we have a second severe weather warning for the Drakensberg Mountains. We expect blizzards and there could be large snowdrifts in some areas. Keep an eye on our website for updates on that if you are thinking of travelling through the mountains tomorrow. That's all from me for now. We'll be back for another weather update at 10 p.m.

🔊 T1, p. 21, Exs 1 & 2

1 A: Hello.
   B: Hello ... it's Amy, isn't it? From the German course?
   A: That's right. Hi, Barry. I haven't seen you in ages.
   B: No, I haven't been coming to class because I've been really busy.
   A: So what are you doing here?
   B: Ah well, I'm going on a sailing trip next week and I need to get a GPS for my boat. This is the best shop in the city. Are you interested in sailing too?
   A: I am, yeah. I come to this shop all the time. They have everything.
   B: Yeah, they do. Right... uhm. I'll see you later, then.
   A: Nice to see you. Bye!
2 C: OK, now just relax, dear. We're here.
   D: Hurry. I think the baby's going to come at any moment.
   C: It's all OK. Look, the nurses are all ready for you. Oh, and it's Janet who will be delivering the baby. That's good news, isn't it?
   D: Janet... She delivered Mike and Charlie. She's delivered all our kids...
   C: Yeah, so it's OK... Everything's under control.
   D: Carlton... I'm so pleased I married you.
   C: I love you too, darling. Now just keep calm. We'll get through this.
3 E: Miriam, can I have a word?
   F: Sure, Lee. What's up?
   E: I'm just preparing the conference room for the meeting with our new clients.
   F: Uh-huh.
   E: It's just... I know the meeting is important but I'm not feeling well.
   F: Oh. What's wrong?
   E: I had a vaccination yesterday, and I've been feeling sick all day.
   F: Well, you go home and rest. I'll look after the meeting.
   E: Oh, thanks Miriam.
   F: Would you like a glass of water or something? You look very white.
4 G: Excuse me! Hello!
   H: Yes?
   G: Hi, er, I wonder if you can help me. We're trying to find the theme park.
   H: Ah... You're in the wrong part of town. You need to drive down this road...
   G: Yes...
   H: And then take North Road. It's the third left, I think.
   G: Is it a long way away?
   H: Maybe another five kilometres.
   G: Right. Thank you very much for your help!
   H: No problem. Enjoy yourselves!
5 I: I can't believe that we lost that match!
   J: They just played better than us. Forget it, we have another game tomorrow. What do you want to eat – one of these sandwiches? Don't worry. I'll pay.
   I: Er, yeah, OK. Thanks. And some orange juice please. You know, I think we should have won the game. Harry and Pamela haven't been playing as long as us.
   I: But they never give up. They keep trying to win, right to the end.
   J: Mm, well, I suppose you're right. Thanks for this, by the way.
   I: That's OK. I have to do something for my tennis partner, don't I!

🔊 4.1, p. 26, Exs 1 & 2

A: So, Chris, tell us about your work here in Macau... First of all, err, how did you become a tattooist?
B: Well, it's simple, really. My father and my grandfather were both tattoo artists, so it's kind of a family business... I say tattoo artist, because tattooing is a real art. You need talent and patience, you know, like any artist.
A: And are tattoos very popular here?
B: Yes, they've been becoming more popular in recent years, but... they're still quite controversial. In the past, many people associated tattoos with criminals and thought they were a bad thing. Even today, if you go for a job interview or something, you might need to cover up your tattoo... Obviously, I really like tattoos, though, all the different styles and designs...
A: Yeah, of course. Is there anything you dislike about your job, though?
B: Well... sometimes dealing with clients is difficult. Often people come and ask for a particular tattoo, but they haven't really thought about what they want. Just this morning I spoke to a guy about his tattoo design and he changed his mind twice while he was talking to me! I refuse to tattoo people if they don't know exactly what they want.
A: Hmm, that makes sense. Do you do a lot of different designs?
B: Yeah, definitely.
A: And which are the most popular?
B: Mmm, many people want Chinese characters. And, er, animal tattoos are very popular at the moment, too. In Chinese tradition, these animals have special meanings. A tattoo of a rabbit represents luck, for example. A tattoo of a monkey represents a fun or a lively person.
A: Right. I guess tattoos often say something about a person's character, or identity...
B: Yeah, I think so. Tattoos are a form of expression. And I enjoy helping people to change their look... I see myself as part of a tradition going back thousands of years and, you know, that makes me feel proud.
A: Well, thanks Chris, for talking to me about your work. It's been really interesting to find out...

🔊 5.2, p. 32, Ex 1

1 A: Where to then?
   B: Well, we don't actually know. Do you know anywhere good to eat round here?
   A: Well, yes. I could take you to Brick Lane. Do you like spicy food?
   B: Yes, I do. Very much.
   A: I can take you to a great restaurant. It serves the best Bangladeshi food you've ever eaten.
   B: That sounds perfect! Let's go there, then.
   A: Right you are.
2 C: Time for a break?
   D: Yeah. I'm exhausted! I don't know how we're going to get this presentation done in time for the board meeting. We'll be working on it all night!

83

Selected Transcripts

C: Well let's have 15 minutes break. I really need a coffee! Mmm... and one of those chocolate doughnuts from the cafeteria...
D: Yeah, I'm really hungry! Let's go then.

3 E: Can I take your order?
F: Er. Yes. I'd like the vegetarian lasagne, please.
E: Good choice. It comes with salad, or French fries.
F: Oh, err, salad, please.
E: And to drink?
F: Just water.
E: Still or sparkling?
F: Uhm... sparkling.
E: Perfect. It'll be about 15 minutes, OK?

4 G: Mm, they've got ice cream! Can I have an ice cream?
H: Not until you've had your main course.
G: But I want ice cream!
H: Yes, and you can have some dessert once you've eaten your vegetables.
G: Oh, but...
H: William...
G: Oh all right.

5 I: Ladies and gentlemen. We've all had a busy morning, so we'll have a break now for lunch. After lunch, we'll continue looking round the old town.
J: Thanks Zahra, that was a lovely morning. The city is extraordinary... And this restaurant looks great, too. What do you recommend for lunch?
I: I'll be having the chicken couscous. It's very good here.
J: What's it like?
I: It's cooked with apricots and cinnamon, so it tastes quite sweet and it's very mild. Try it!
J: Mm, I think I will.

6.1, p. 35, Ex 6

I-A-N – comedian, musician
E-R, O-R – actor, composer, director, illustrator, producer
I-S-T – cartoonist, dramatist
I-C – critic

6.2, p. 38, Exs 1-3

1 A: Oh no!
B: What's wrong, Lucy?
A: I don't know where my DVD of Twilight is...
B: Twilight?
A: Yeah, you know, the vampire film? With Robert Pattinson. You know the one.
B: Yeah, of course I know it. It's a great film.
A: Well, I really need to find it. Monika's coming round this evening and I promised her that we'd watch it.
B: Oh, right, yeah. It would be awful if you didn't have it.

A: It must be here somewhere ...
B: You've got so many DVDs, Lucy. Isn't there something else you could watch?
A: Not really. Monika really wants to see Twilight.
B: Mmm, well, it is a timeless classic.
A: Finally! Here it is! Hey, Carrie, why don't you join us tonight? We're just going to chill out and watch the film.
B: Oh, err... I'm really sorry, but I can't. I've got loads to do. But thanks, Lucy.

2 C: Have you seen this photo, Jose?
D: Dominoes in Cuba! That takes me back.
C: And these guys playing it are young too. They're our age.
D: People play it all the time back in Cuba. They're very competitive. They play really fast and they keep saying 'come on, come on, it's not chess!'
C: Do you miss Cuba?
D: Yeah. I haven't been there for years.
C: That must be really hard for you. But I'm sure you'll go back there one day.
D: Yeah, well ,... Let me show you these... my dominoes.
C: Oh wow. They're beautiful! Are they handmade?
D: Yeah. I carved them myself. I love doing this kind of woodwork, in my spare time.
C: Well you're a real artist, Jose. These look as if they were made by a professional.
D: Thanks. So shall we play?
C: Sure, yeah. I'd love to have a go!
D: OK, great. But I warn you, I'm quite competitive!

T2, p. 41, Exs 1 & 2

A: Hello. I'm Jake –
B: And I'm Leila. Welcome to our podcast. Every week we take a look at computer games that interest us. And this week, it's –
A: Cooking Mama World Kitchen. Leila, give us the background.
B: Cooking Mama is part of a series of games. The first one came out in 2006 for the Nintendo DS console, and the latest version is Cooking Mama World Kitchen for the Wii.
A: So what's special about the Wii version?
B: Well you can now use your controller to chop vegetables and slice food. You also use it to boil ingredients or grill them on the barbecue.
A: It works really well on the Wii, doesn't it? I thought the game play was excellent.
B: There were a few little problems, and the motion sensor didn't capture every movement perfectly, but yeah, in general, it works very well indeed.
A: What was your favourite thing about the game?

B: The graphics are terrific. They are just brilliant on the Wii, and they're now in 3D too.
A: I also thought that the character of Mama was hilarious. Some of the things she says are just crazy.
B: So what was your favourite recipe?
A: I absolutely loved making the chocolate chip cookies. In fact, I then used the recipe in real life and made a box of them for my friends.
B: My favourite was a disaster. I was making a burger and it fell on the floor. Then Mama's dog ate it!
A: I remember that! That was pretty funny. So, who would you recommend this game for, Leila?
B: You can learn it very quickly so I think it's fun for a party with your friends.
A: I agree. It's also great for kids because it's not violent like a shoot 'em up or something like that.
B: So thumbs up for Cooking Mama. Four stars from me.
A: Oh, I give it five.
B: Jake, you're so predictable!
A: What can I say? It was lots of fun.
B: OK, thanks everyone, and don't forget to tune into our next podcast on Saturday. Bye for now!

7.2, p. 46, Exs 2 & 3

1 A: Hello there, madam. How can I help you?
B: Please can you tell me when my visa will be ready? I've been waiting here for nearly three hours.
A: I'm very sorry, but I can't answer your question. You'll have to wait until one of the visa officials can see you.
B: I'm afraid that just isn't good enough. I need to know what's going on. If this isn't sorted out quickly, I'm going to have to make a formal complaint.
A: OK, wait here one moment please. I'll try and find out what the problem is.
B: Thank you.

2 C: Oh no, I don't believe this!
D: What's happened? What's in that envelope?
C: They've sent my tax return form back... again! But I'm sure I filled everything in correctly. It took me hours to sort out the problem the last time they returned it. I really don't have time for this! Why do they make these forms so complicated?
D: Look, don't worry, darling. It's probably just a simple mistake. Let's sit down and look at it together. If you get all the documents ready, I'll make us a cup of coffee. We'll sort it out.
C: OK, thanks Richard.

3 E: Good evening, sir. Can I see your ticket, please?
   F: Oh, of course. Here you are.
   E: Thank you. And sorry, but would you mind turning your MP3 player off, please? This is the quiet carriage, so we ask passengers not to use mobile phones or listen to music. There is a sign here.
   F: Oh, OK. I'm sorry, I didn't realise. I didn't know what the sign meant.
   E: That's no problem at all. If you'd prefer to listen to music, you could move to another carriage. It's up to you.
   F: Right, thanks.
4 G: Excuse me, officer. What's going on here?
   H: There's been a gas leak inside number 24. It may be dangerous, so we're asking everyone to wait outside until the problem has been resolved.
   G: What? But my office is inside that building. I have an important meeting in an hour. I need to go inside and prepare!
   H: I'm very sorry, but I'm going to have to ask you to wait here. Engineers from the gas company are dealing with the problem at the moment. I'm sure the work will be finished within the next hour.
   G: Right. And what am I supposed to do 'til then? Honestly, this is just ridiculous...

8.2, p. 52, Exs 1 & 2

1 A: Have you seen Mary? We're supposed to be having a meeting about the Jaycott trial.
   B: No, sorry. By the way, have you heard that she's leaving?
   A: Really, when?
   B: Next week apparently... Mm, that reminds me, she borrowed some money from me last week. I must get it back before she goes.
   A: Good luck with that! She's so forgetful.
   B: Huh, yeah. Incidentally, if you do see her, can you remind her that we're going for dinner this evening?
2 C: Guess what? I'm going to be in court next week – I'm on a jury.
   D: Oh really? That should be interesting.
   C: Yes, I think so. It's quite a long trial though – I've had to take two weeks off work.
   D: Talking about trials, did you see the report about vandalism on the news last night?
   C: No, what happened?
3 E: Right, I've finished my report on the burglary at the school so I'm heading off now.
   F: OK, have a good evening. Before I forget, can you come in a bit early tomorrow? We've got a lot to cover.
   E: All right. I'll try to be here by 8. Changing the subject, have you heard if there's a date for the arson court case?
   F: Not yet. I'll let you know as soon as I hear anything.
   E: Thanks, that would be great. Right then, I should go – I don't want to miss my train. See you tomorrow.
   F: Bye!

8.3, p. 52, Ex 1

Ladies and gentlemen, can I have your attention please? Owing to vandalism on the railway line, trains will not be running from Canterbury to London this morning. Passengers for the 9.35 London service should wait in the station car park for the replacement bus service. The buses will depart at about 10.15 and should arrive at London Victoria at about 12.00. Trains from Canterbury to Dover are not affected. Please see signs in the station for more information. I'm very sorry for this change to your service, but the problem was only discovered this morning by the local police. We hope that all services will be back to normal by late afternoon.

9.2, p. 58, Ex 1

1 A: I'm sorry sir, but I can't let you into the swimming pool without a swimming cap.
   B: What do you mean?
   A: It's a rule. You have to have a cap in the swimming pool.
   B: I don't believe this! I've just walked for thirty minutes to get here, and now I can't get in!
   A: We do sell them, sir. You can buy one in the shop.
   B: Right. And how much do they cost?
   A: Only €1.
   B: Fine. I'll do that then.
2 C: Hello?
   D: Hello is that Mariam ... Ahmadi?
   C: Yes, who is this please?
   D: Do you have internet access at home, Ms Ahmadi?
   C: Look, I'm...
   D: If you are interested in changing your internet service provider, we can offer you a special price for the first six months.
   C: I'm very sorry, but I'm not interested...
   D: We can install WiFi throughout your home within 24 hours of signing your contract.
   C: Sorry, but I don't want to change my internet service! This is the third call I've had today.
   D: Our offer is extremely competitive and if you would -
   C: I'm sorry. I'm not interested in all these deals. Goodbye.
3 E: What's up, Suresh?
   F: I just checked my lottery numbers online. I use the same ones every week...
   E: Oh right. Did you win anything this time?
   F: No such luck. I would have won £50, but... I didn't buy a ticket!
   E: Oh no! Why not?
   F: I went to the shops yesterday to buy a good luck card for my little sister. She's taking her final university exams next week. I was going to buy a lottery ticket at the same time, but I completely forgot.
   E: Poor you!
4 G: Hey Joe, what's wrong?
   H: Someone stole my skateboard.
   G: Oh no!
   H: The thing that makes me really angry is that it was another skateboarder who took it. I left it in the road to take a phone call. It was a place where lots of us go skateboarding. It wasn't at school or at the sports centre or somewhere like that. It's so annoying!
   G: Was it worth a lot of money?
   H: Yeah, it was quite valuable. I won it in a competition at the skate shop.
   G: Oh, poor you. That's so unlucky.
   H: Yeah, and now I'll have to get a job so I can save for a new one.

T3, p. 61, Exs 1 & 2

Good evening, and welcome to Police Report where we keep you up to date with crime in the local area.
First of all, we have the arrest of four protestors who tried to enter the nuclear power station illegally on Sunday night. The protestors, all aged between 17 and 19, argue that nuclear power is untrustworthy and dangerous. The police released them on Monday without further charges.
Residents of New Town have taken action against vandals in their area, following a series of criminal acts. Shops, bus stops and even apartment buildings have all been damaged in the last month. A new law has been passed which allows the police to give anyone committing this type of crime an immediate fine of between 50 and 100 dollars. Next, a warning to anyone out there who downloads films from the internet – the government can now stop internet access for anyone using pirate websites. Bear in mind that police will only give a single caution before stopping the internet connection. Around 300 connections have already been closed. Police have now confirmed that

Selected Transcripts

no one was injured in yesterday's fire at Good Hope High School. However, the school believes that it will need to spend over $10,000 to repair the damage caused to its indoor tennis courts, where the fire was started. The principal said that she was 'very disappointed' by the irresponsible behaviour of the students who started the fire. Finally, a funny story to start the weekend. An unlucky thief named Roger Churchill chose the wrong house to rob last Tuesday night. While Churchill was stealing the DVD player and the TV, he was caught by the house's owner, Mr Bruce Twining. Mr Twining is an ex-professional boxer and he held Churchill in the living room until the police arrived. Churchill has now been sentenced to 18 months' community service. That's all for now from Police Report. Keep your eyes open and keep safe.

🔊 10.1, p. 63, Ex 8

1. A lot of food and drink packaging is made of polystyrene.
2. The old temple in the town centre is made of beautiful white marble.
3. Copper is often used to make electricity cables.
4. Bottles of wine or oil often have tops made of cork.
5. There are too many ugly grey concrete buildings in this city.
6. The walls of the villa are decorated with painted ceramic tiles.

🔊 10.2, p. 66, Ex 1

When you're shopping on the high street do you fork out a lot more money than you expected? Do you know which products are the biggest rip off? Today we speak to retail specialist Huang Wen, who'll tell us how to save money at the shops.

🔊 10.3, p. 66, Ex 2

A: When you're shopping on the high street do you fork out a lot more money than you expected? Do you know which products are the biggest rip off? Today we speak to retail specialist Huang Wen, who'll tell us how to save money at the shops. Huang, welcome.
B: Hi Pippa.
A: So Huang, what are the biggest rip offs at the shops?
B: Actually the biggest rip off often comes before you get to the shops. The price of train tickets changes a lot during the day and there are a lot of special deals, too. But often the staff at the railway station don't tell you about the offers.
A: So how do we get the best prices? Look online?
B: No, it's actually best to call the railway company to find the cheapest train tickets.
A: OK... And when we get to the shops, what should we look out for?
B: Err... the sales! The price you pay for clothes, for example, is usually several times their real value. It's best to wait until the sales to buy them.
A: But there are never clothes in my size in the sales.
B: If you want to get something in the sales, you have to go on the first day. Ask someone in the shop what day the sales begin. Here's a tip – sales often begin on a Thursday when most people are at work.
A: Right, OK, I'll remember that. What other products are overpriced?
B: Imagine the scene. You've been shopping all day for a new leather sofa. You've neither found the right colour nor the right design. You're exhausted. So what do you do?
A: I usually go to a café with my friends.
B: Exactly, and this is where the real rip off happens. How much do you pay for a cup of coffee? £3?
A: Yeah... Something like that.
B: Right. Well the real cost of the coffee is about 10 pence a cup! So what are you paying for?
A: Well, the staff I suppose... and the big shiny coffee machines...
B: That's true but with a 1000% profit, the café soon pays for all of that!
A: OK, they're making a lot of money, but I don't want to give up my coffee!
B: Neither do I, but shop around. Local cafes usually offer cheaper drinks than the big chains.
A: OK, Huang, thanks for your advice. Now if you'd like to call in and ask Huang any questions, our number is...

🔊 11.2, p. 72, Exs 1 & 2

A: We've all been there... There's something wrong with your computer and you can't fix it. You phone for help, and... Many of us have had frustrating experiences with computer helplines. But how does it feel on the other end of the phone? Today on Insiders, I'm talking to an ex-call centre operator, Nikhil. Welcome to the programme, Nikhil.
B: Thank you.
A: So first of all, how did you get your job in the call centre?
B: Well, the job came from nowhere, really. I studied computer science at university, and one evening, I met this guy outside the library on the campus. He gave me a leaflet from a call centre – they were looking for computer science students to work for their IT helpline.
A: So you got in contact with them?
B: Yeah. I was just the person they were looking for. I could work evenings and weekends, I knew about computers... Oh, and most of all, I was happy to work for very little money, because I was a student!
A: And how did you keep motivated? It must be very boring.
B: Actually, the work was pretty stressful! In the call centre, there's a computer on the wall and it, err, it tells you how many callers are waiting. It also tells you how long each call lasts. So, um, everyone in the office can see exactly how well you're doing, all the time!
A: Hmm, that does sound stressful! Did you get on with your colleagues, then?
B: Absolutely. They were all really good fun, and my boss was laid-back... unlike the customers! Some of them were really difficult, and others asked really silly questions!
A: Like what?
B: Err, well, one person phoned up because of a problem with his handheld games player. He was really angry because he'd only bought it a week before, and it had stopped working. After half an hour, we discovered the problem – he'd never recharged it. Honestly, you can make your technology as intuitive as you like, but some people will never understand it! Another lady said she couldn't install a certain program onto her computer... After 20 minutes, we found out the problem... She hadn't bought the program and she didn't have the disk!
A: Really?
B: One person told me their computer wouldn't boot up. I told him what to do, but nothing worked. In the end, I asked, 'is your computer on? Have you turned it on?' And he said, 'Oh, I need to turn my computer on, do I?'
A: How do you keep calm in situations like that?
B: To be honest, I just thought about the money! I was a poor student, remember? And most of the time it was funny. In fact, it was useful because now I work for a software company. When I'm designing software, it's useful to know about the problems people have with technology!
A: Nikhil, that's all we have time for. It's been lovely talking to you.
B: And to you.

12.2, p. 78, Exs 1 & 2

A: Hi, Anna speaking.
B: Anna, hi, it's me.
A: Stuart! Great to hear from you! How are you doing? Where are you this week?
B: I'm in Tromsø, in Norway.
A: Oh yeah, you're writing a feature about the aurora borealis, aren't you? Have you seen them, the Northern Lights?
B: Yeah, we saw them last night. It was amazing, a once in a lifetime experience.
A: Hmm. It's a hard life being a travel journalist, isn't it?
B: Yeah, well... Um, actually, Anna, I need your help.
A: Oh, OK. What's up?
B: I need to write my blog for the magazine website, but... my laptop's broken. I can't get it fixed until the weekend and there are no internet cafes here!
A: You're joking! What are you going to do?
B: Well... I was wondering, err... Can you write the blog post for me? Just this once.
A: Oh Stuart ... Well I suppose, if you can't get to a computer... Let me get a pen and I'll write some notes... OK, ready.
B: Right, so I'm staying near the Sandvannet Lake in Norway and we've come to see the aurora borealis. The first night, in the dead of night, we drove out into the woods. It was quite exciting, but... unfortunately, we didn't see the lights because it was too cloudy.
A: OK... Carry on.
B: So, err, we went to the woods again last night. And then... we finally saw them. These bright, moving lights in the sky. Honestly, Anna, it's breath-taking, like something from a Science Fiction film!
A: OK. So why do they have such a strange name?
B: The aurora borealis? It's because they're named after Aurora, the Roman goddess of the dawn.
A: And what do they look like?
B: Well they're like waves of light in the sky. They're usually green or red, but I saw lots of other colours too. I couldn't believe my eyes...
A: And, in the blog, don't you normally include some travel information for the readers? I mean, when can they see the lights?
B: Well, it's winter now, but the best times are spring or autumn... Look Anna, I'm really sorry but I have to go – thanks so much for helping me with this. You're a life saver!
A: Hmm, well – you owe me.
B: Definitely! Thanks again, and speak soon.
A: OK. Bye Stuart!

T4, p. 81, Exs 1 & 2

A: This is Jeremy Price. It's time for the last afternoon slot on travel tips. We're here with Malikah, who'll be talking to us about her recent trip to Petra, in Jordan. Malikah, welcome.
B: Hi Jeremy.
A: So what did you think of Petra?
B: It was fantastic. We all know the temple in the rock from photos, and from the Indiana Jones films, and you know the films are good fun, but actually visiting Petra is incredible. It's an awe-inspiring place.
A: What is there around the temple?
B: Well, Petra itself is a very large site with many ancient buildings. To visit it properly, you need two or even three days.
A: And how do you travel around? By jeep?
B: No, that's too noisy for me. Instead, I suggest hiring a horse!
A: A horse?
B: Yeah, you can ride all round the site.
A: Amazing. Now, what about guides?
B: Personally, I think it's good to get a guide. It's a great way to meet local people. And don't worry about prices – they're very fair in Jordan. You can get by on a few dollars a day.
A: I agree. So what's the best time to visit Petra?
B: Go at sunrise when there aren't many people there. It's breath-taking. Sadly, there are a lot of tourists in Petra now, and in the afternoon it's just too crowded.
A: And very hot, I imagine?
B: Yes, it can be incredibly hot. You should bring lots of water, whatever time of day you visit.
A: OK ... What about accommodation in Petra? What's that like?
B: Well, last time, I actually stayed in a Bedouin camp – I'd really recommend it. I found out about it online. I went with a tour group and everyone was really friendly. Luckily, we didn't travel by camel or anything like that – I'm not a fan of camel rides!
A: So what was the camp like?
B: When we walked into our tents ... well, they were beautiful. And camping in the desert was amazing – if you looked out of the tent in the dead of night, you could see so many stars. The view was stunning.
A: Mm, it sounds like a once-in-a-lifetime experience. Well, Malikah, that's all we have time for today, but we'll be speaking to you again soon, after your next trip! Thanks for chatting to us today.
B: Jeremy, thank you. It's always a pleasure to come on the show.

Track listing

Transcript	Content	Track
1.1	Page 3, Exercise 6	1
1.2	Page 6, Listening, Exercises 1 & 2	2
2.1	Page 12, Functional language, Exercise 1	3
2.2	Page 12, Listening, Exercises 1 & 2	4
3.1	Page 15, Exercise 6	5
3.2	Page 18, Listening, Exercises 1 & 2	6
T1	Page 21, Progress test 1, Listening	7
4.1	Page 26, Listening, Exercises 1 & 2	8
5.1	Page 29, Exercise 5	9
5.2	Page 32, Listening, Exercise 1	10
6.1	Page 35, Exercise 6	11
6.2	Page 38, Listening, Exercises 1-3	12
T2	Page 41, Progress test 2, Listening	13
7.1	Page 43, Exercise 5	14
7.2	Page 46, Listening, Exercises 2 & 3	15
8.1	Page 49, Exercise 6	16
8.2	Page 52, Functional language, Exercises 1 & 2	17
8.3	Page 52, Listening, Exercise 1	18
9.1	Page 55, Exercise 5	19
9.2	Page 58, Listening, Exercise 1	20
T3	Page 61, Progress test 3, Listening	21
10.1	Page 63, Exercise 8	22
10.2	Page 66, Listening, Exercise 1	23
10.3	Page 66, Listening, Exercise 2	24
11.1	Page 69, Exercise 5	25
11.2	Page 72, Listening, Exercises 1 & 2	26
12.1	Page 75, Exercise 7	27
12.2	Page 78, Listening, Exercises 1 & 2	28
T4	Page 81, Progress test 4, Listening	29